The Age of the Person

SOCIETY IN THE TWENTIETH CENTURY

The Age of

the Person

by DIETRICH VON OPPEN

translated by FRANK CLARKE

foreword by JAMES LUTHER ADAMS

Fortress Press   Philadelphia

This book is a translation of *Das personale Zeitalter. Formen und Grundlagen gesellschaftlichen Lebens im 20. Jahrhundert*, copyright 1960 by Verlagsgemeinschaft Burckhardthaus- und Kreuz-Verlag GmbH. in Stuttgart, Germany.

Library of Congress Catalog Card Number 71–84536

2025B69   Printed in U.S.A.   1-284

Contents

Foreword

The uniqueness of this volume by the eminent sociologist of the Theological Faculty of Marburg University is immediately suggested by its title, *The Age of the Person*. Analysts of modern society have been prone to speak of our century as the age of the impersonal, of technology, specialization, the mass man — epithets that bring into bold relief what has been viewed as a process of dehumanization, depersonalization. To be sure, these analysts have presupposed some positive conception of the authentically human, but they have defined it largely in terms of its absence. Although Dr. von Oppen does not discuss the concepts of twentieth-century society which differ radically from his own, one needs to bear them in mind if one is to grasp the full import of his analysis. Of the major views of this sort, a few of which we may consider by way of example, it would not be misleading to say that they delineate the modern period as in some sense a Fall.

Ferdinand Tönnies viewed the medieval social order as a group of "communities" each held together by a complex of affective states, habits, and traditions expressing loyalty, honor, and friendship; it was followed by a congeries of "associations" concerned with limited practical ends and possessing a high degree of fissiparous individualism, contractualism, competition, egoism, rationality, and calculation — in short, of "impersonality." There is more than a touch of nostalgia for the past in Tönnies, for the present society of "associations" represents a falling away from the original, affectional "community." In the outlook of Karl Marx one can see an anticipation of Tönnies' conception, though for Marx the causal relationship is reversed: the loss of community is the consequence of capitalism.

Emile Durkheim described the transition from a "mechanical" to an "organic" society as a transition from a communal authority to a threatening anarchy of values. He saw the consequence of the transition to be the submersion of persons in a mass of atomistic rudderless individuals.

Max Weber presented a tragic view of the course of modern culture. He saw the emergence of rationality in its emancipation from mere traditionalism to be initially a move in the direction of a new depth of meaning with respect to goals, but rationality has deteriorated into a routinized, dehumanizing, conscienceless passion for efficiency of means, whatever ends are sought. Beginning with a profound religious conception of vocation, modern man is now enclosed in the "iron cage" of specialization "without spirit . . . , a nullity that imagines it has attained a level of civilization never before achieved." Tragedy issues from a noble flaw, and it drives towards depersonalization, towards alienation from the creative forces of life.

David Riesman marks out a similar course, though without exhibiting nostalgia for the past. The "inner-direction" of the past was the internalized authority of the fathers, whereas the "other-direction" of the present is bound by radar to the externalized authority of the peer group; both "inner-direction" and "outer-direction" are "outer-directed." Riesman looks for a different kind of "inner-direction," the inner "gyroscope" of an autonomy that is sufficiently free to possess "the nerve of failure," the courage of "the saving remnant."

None of these analysts, to be sure, paints a completely black picture. Yet for all of them the structure and dominant ethos of contemporary society appear in the main to be a wasteland, and the voice is that of one crying in the wilderness of depersonalization.

Dietrich von Oppen does not view twentieth-century society as a wasteland of depersonalization. Far from it. This does not mean that he ignores the seamy side of contemporary society. Indeed, one can see analogues between his descriptions of this seamy side and those of the analysts mentioned above. Yet he holds that our society not only makes special demands upon the person but also provides structures within which and between which the opportunities for personal responsibility are legion.

In his multidimensional analysis von Oppen places major emphasis upon the emergence in modern society of what he calls "the principle of organization." The characteristically modern organization presents a striking contrast to the traditional, sacrosanct institution: it is completely secularized (in the sense that it does not claim absolute sanction from above or from tradition) and it is flexible, open to structural change in face of changing conditions and sensitivities. Thus the person is set free. He is no longer enclosed within a sacrosanct group. Today "no method of work, no demarcation of authority, no chain of command, and no form of cooperation, is sacred and inviolable." Any such inviolability would bring an end to viability.

The author traces historically the appearance and development of this "principle of organization," showing how in varying ways it has affected the family, the state, the business enterprise, voluntary associations, and even the church. Indeed, the principle appeared first in the church, even if today it is *en retard*. It is precisely in the pluralistic society of modern organizations that the integrity and freedom of the person, and also personal responsibility, become characteristic and indispensable. To compromise the freedom and openness of pluralism is to move in the direction of routinization and ultimately towards totalitarianism. Thus ours is the age of "the person."

But the greater uniqueness of this book appears on another level, where von Oppen identifies the Sermon on the Mount as the source of the principle of organization, and of modern man's decisive recognition of the person and of personal responsibility. This view is unique even among church historians and biblical scholars, who customarily assert that the Gospels specify no particular social-institutional ethics, no preferred social or political philosophy. While Dr. von Oppen would not deny this, he insists that the Sermon on the Mount with its "You have heard that it was said to the men of old . . . . But I say . . ." shakes the foundation of traditional institutions. By bringing them under judgment it relativizes them so that they lose their sacrosanct protection. At the same time it places full responsibility upon the person, who with his integrity before God, his responsibility before God, becomes the fulcrum and even the ground of all human relations — the relation to God, to one's fellowmen, and to oneself. From this beginning the author traces the development of Western society with its many stages and setbacks, the long development for which the Sermon on the Mount is the presupposition.

This summary of the underlying thesis of the book obviously cannot take the place of the author's detailed, and more subtle, presentation. Nor can it give more than a hint of the way in which his extensive account of Western history offers an interpretation different in important respects from the "wasteland interpretations" referred to earlier.

Yet we should indicate briefly too how certain aspects of the presentation relate to the findings of American sociologists of religion. At important junctures the author's account reminds one of Talcott Parsons' description of differentiation as it has developed in the history of Christianity and of modern culture. The indicated interplay of communal and associational elements described by the author bears striking analogy to the findings of Will Herberg and Gerhard Lenski. The theory of pluralism will remind the reader of the writings of A. D. Lindsay (late Master of Balliol College, Oxford) and his forebears. Most important of all is the conception of the Christian "image of man" which William L. Kolb has delineated in its relation to contemporary sociology of religion.

Finally, we should observe that Dr. von Oppen's whole method of analysis, in its preoccupation with the person and with personal responsibility, must be understood in relation to the "transcendental theory of society" adumbrated by his teacher, Helmut Schelsky, sociologist at the University of Münster, a theory that sets man over against society by placing him beyond all social constraints:

> . . . the reflecting subjectivity which no social force can ultimately determine and no social reality ultimately express, the moral conscience which no social reality can ultimately either confirm or refute, the religious faith which is ultimately committed to no social reality, not even itself. What is involved here is a confrontation between "subjective reflection and social constraint" which can be described under the rubric "subjectivity and the institutions."*

The thesis of this book is that personal responsibility cannot be relevant or effective apart from an understanding of the social-institutional milieu, yet "no social force can ultimately determine it." What determines it is the moral conscience before God, as it confronts the enemy: routinization, subjection to "established" institutions, subjection to the law from which the gospel liberates men with "explosive power."

This Protestant ethic is classically depicted in Albrecht Dürer's engraving of the *Knight, Death, and the Devil.* Here the Knight, the Christian Pilgrim, in face of "spooks and phantoms," rides resolutely through the wasteland of rough and dreary scenery, defying Death and the Devil, his eyes on a destination that is still far off at the end of a steep, winding road. For the author of this book the age of the person *coram deo* gives cause for new hope.

JAMES LUTHER ADAMS

* Helmut Schelsky, *Ortsbestimmung der deutschen Soziologie* (Düsseldorf: Eugen Diederichs Verlag, 1959), p. 105.

Translator's Preface

The rendering of technical terms and phrases from one language and national setting to another is always difficult. The editorial staff of Fortress Press has very kindly helped by introducing American terminology at a number of points. Some translator's notes have also been inserted here and there. In a book dealing with social groupings, the terms are necessarily many and diverse. The various German designations of groups — *Verein, Verband,* etc. — are not always easy to render into English, as Ernest Barker noted in the preface to his translation of Otto von Gierke's *Natural Law and the Theory of Society, 1500–1800* (London: Cambridge University Press, 1950), pp. lxxxix–xci. We have not attempted to follow Barker's usage but have simply sought to find what seemed the nearest English equivalent in each case. Consistency has remained one of our goals, but, as in all translations, different contexts may require different renderings. Clarity and general intelligibility, rather than specialist use of technical terms, seemed appropriate criteria in the translation of a book addressed to the general reader.

Introduction:

Approach and Method

The aim of this volume is to give an overview of the structures in which human corporate life is at present organized. An attempt will be made to draw a few guidelines through the bewildering multiplicity of phenomena in our communal life.

Such an attempt is nothing new. Recent years and decades have seen the appearance of numerous studies interpreting the present age on the basis of critical analysis of our society. We mention only Hans Freyer's *Theorie des gegenwärtigen Zeitalters*,[1] Karl Mannheim's *Diagnosis of our Time*,[2] David Riesman's *The Lonely Crowd*,[3] and Peter Drucker's *Landmarks of Tomorrow*.[4] Common to these and other works, however, is that they treat the question of the position and significance of the Christian faith in the modern world peripherally, if at all, instead of putting it in the center. The latter task has been undertaken, as far as the present writer knows, only by Hans-Dietrich Wendland in his widely read work *Die*

[1] Hans Freyer, *Theorie des gegenwärtigen Zeitalters* (Stuttgart: Deutsche Verlags-Anstalt, 1955).
[2] Karl Mannheim, *Diagnosis of Our Time: Wartime Essays of a Sociologist* (New York: Humanities Press, 1962).
[3] David Riesman *et al.*, *The Lonely Crowd: A Study of the Changing American Character* (New Haven: Yale University Press, 1950; abr. ed., New York: Doubleday & Co., 1953).
[4] Peter Drucker, *Landmarks of Tomorrow* (New York: Harper & Row, 1959).

Kirche in der modernen Gesellschaft.[5] The present volume is based on the conviction that this question is crucial and indispensable to an understanding of modern society. In analyses of our age there can be, in the long run, no justification for relegating this question to the periphery or for neglecting it altogether, for in that case essential forces and fundamental processes are inevitably lost sight of.

Now, the constitution of society in any period is a living and extremely complex affair, and no overview as brief as the present work can claim to disclose *the* final view of it, or to reveal *the* precise structure. All that is ever possible is to suggest several possible approaches, and thus to offer an overall view within certain limited perspectives which over-emphasize some aspects while causing others to recede or disappear completely. One cannot strive for anything more than to plumb as deeply as possible toward the center, there to find a point of departure, and in this way to disclose as much as possible.

It will be useful, here at the outset, to give a clear account of the path that we propose to follow, so as to facilitate the reader's participation as well as his criticism. Our first postulate is that we are today confronted by a single great process of industrialization which, by degrees and in a variety of forms, is laying hold of the whole world. "Industrialization" is as inadequate and unsatisfying a designation for this process as is "modernization." Both terms are used for want of a better one; the right name for this age of ours has yet to be found. In any case, it is becoming increasingly evident that behind the facade of divergent social and political doctrines all five continents are growing increasingly similar.

Secondly, we have thus already established that we are here confronted with a process, not with a fixed state of affairs. The powerful movement that keeps our world gasping makes it unavoidable that we view our age as one of movement, that is, as history. This is a process that stretches far back into the past

[5] Hans-Dietrich Wendland, *Die Kirche in der modernen Gesellschaft. Entscheidungsfragen für das kirchliche Handeln im Zeitalter der Massenwelt* (2d ed. rev.; Hamburg: Furche-Verlag, 1958).

and that in its present state represents only a transition, a single phase. The second postulate of our presentation, then, is that the present age stands in the stream of history.

Thirdly, there is the striking fact that the process of industrialization originated, not just anywhere in the world, but in a very specific area, namely, among the Christian peoples of the West, or, to be more precise, in the area evangelized by Rome and stamped with its imprint. This is common knowledge. The question therefore suggests itself: What inner connections underlie this outward concatenation of circumstances? And we are thus brought back to the challenge voiced at the start, that we inquire about the part played by the Christian faith in the development of Western society. At the same time, this historical question is pointed toward its real import, for the historical thought of the West was kindled by the Old and New Testament view of history as directed toward a purpose or goal. This can be seen even today in the fact that we still reckon time in our era from the birth of Christ.

There are, then, just a few major and generally recognized facts from which we would start our investigation: the growing unification of the world, the historical movement in which we stand, and the importance of the Christian faith as one of the crucial factors in the creation and fashioning of our society. It remains to be seen what light an approach based on these facts can throw on our confused age.

Part I

The Christian Roots

of Modern Society

1

Institution and Person in the

Sermon on the Mount

The structures of modern society, which our whole generation is at pains to understand and master, originated for the
most part in central and western Europe during the last century and a half. It is customary now to refer to this critical
chapter in human history as the "Industrial Revolution." It
certainly was a revolution, even though this conventional term
may not be quite satisfactory. The period has often been said
to compare in significance with only one other in the history of
mankind, namely, the transition from nomadic and hunting
cultures to the establishment of agrarian settlements, which
took place in our latitudes about five thousand years ago, at
the transition from the Paleolithic to the Neolithic Age.
Whether this comparison is legitimate or not, the fact remains
that the rise of the machine age has confronted mankind with
unprecedented situations and problems, and the span of a
hundred and fifty years has hardly afforded sufficient time in
which to cope with them.

It is simply not true, however, that the turn of the nineteenth century witnessed a sudden and abrupt revolution.
What happened is that about that time a long process of historical development reached its climax. And when one looks

for the origins and motive powers of this process, one comes not only to the impulses emanating from ancient Greece and Rome, but first and foremost to the Christian faith. By this we do not mean simply the superficial fact that this development took place in the Christian West, and that the West still reckons time with reference to the inception of its faith. It can be demonstrated in detail that — and to what extent — a revolutionary and world-transforming power emanated from the Christian gospel. It is the thesis of this book that the world of today cannot be understood apart from a recognition of this revolutionary power. Before turning to the consideration of historical and sociological factors, we must therefore give our attention to the gospel itself. For here is to be found a decisive key to understanding, not only the direction that affairs have taken in the West, but also the contemporary world as such.

It has been frequently and vigorously emphasized, for example, by Hans-Dietrich Wendland, that the New Testament contains no program for social reform, that it neither depicts nor prescribes any "Christian society." That is correct, and any interpreter who ignores the fact is bound to go astray. But it is equally erroneous to think that the New Testament concerns itself only with that which is within a man, some inner condition that is of no importance or consequence for the structures of his outward life.

There is, in fact, a third possibility: the gospel has put the believer into a completely new kind of relationship to the world, and hence also to the structures of his life — to the family, the state, and those in authority; and as a result of this new relationship these structures have themselves been transformed. The brand-new complex of social structures which is our modern world came into being only during the course of a long historical development. And it may well be that this world appears to us so confused and incomprehensible precisely because we are no longer aware of its origin, and hence of the regulative principle that secretly underlies it.

While the new relationship of the believer to the structures of society is to be seen throughout the whole gospel, it is expressed most concisely and clearly in the Sermon on the Mount. In these chapters of Matthew's Gospel — which probably represent a later compilation of sayings that had been transmitted as independent logia — the affirmations most significant for our present purpose are given in a particularly compact and explicit, indeed, almost systematic form. In the following attempt to explicate these affirmations we make no claim to having opened the way to *the* correct interpretation. The Sermon on the Mount, like the whole gospel, is a living thing, of which there can be, within the sphere of human history, no final, "correct," and exhaustive interpretation. One can only hope to approach the Sermon from a new direction, and on the basis of new questions to gain new answers.

There is one question, however, to which the Sermon on the Mount does offer a particularly clear answer: In what way did the gospel so fundamentally and permanently change man's relationship to the external structures of his life as to produce a radical transformation in those structures themselves? For, we must repeat, the gospel did effect a revolution in human history, a revolution whose character and direction are spelled out very specifically in the words of the Sermon on the Mount.

The "Law" as Embodiment of the Institution

The substance of the Sermon on the Mount is the overcoming of "the law" — that is, the strictly institutionalized national code of the Jewish people in the late Hellenistic period. This "law" first appears in some of the central commands of the ancient Torah itself (Matt. 5:21–48) under the rubric: "You have heard that it was said to the men of old . . . ." It also appears in the mention made of selected aspects of life lived under the norms of these commands, specifically with respect to religious ritual (6:1–18) and "civic" conduct in general (6:19—7:5). On closer examination, however, we see that what we encounter here is something more than simply the particular, historically unique form of the Jewish religion of the law. If we take into account all the various norms of conduct that are here called into question, what emerges is, point for point and feature for feature, the commonly accepted picture of a human institution as such. Whenever men live together on a continuing basis, these features must inevitably appear in one form or another. A brief glance at the text of the Sermon will confirm this, and will show that the way in which it comes to grips with a fundamental reality of human life has a significance that transcends time and place.

The series of sayings begins, significantly enough, with the preservation of life, something that every social order is basically concerned to effect and guarantee: "You shall not kill; and whoever kills shall be liable to judgment" (5:21). The statute sets up the protective guarantee, and an institutional organ, the court, enforces it as may be necessary.

The situation is similar in the case of marriage, which, as the source of new life, is another matter that necessarily receives attention in every human society: "You shall not commit adultery" (5:27), and, "Whoever divorces his wife, let him give her a certificate of divorce" (5:31). The statute establishes the permanence of the relationship between man and wife, and provides, in cases of necessity, for the dissolution of a union that has become intolerable.

Integrity in statements of a serious nature and reliability in voluntary contracts are fundamental requisites of corporate life. These are established by fixed and solemn formulas for making statements, and in extreme cases are guaranteed by a religious form of oath: "You shall not swear falsely, but shall perform to the Lord what you have sworn" (5:33).

If the social order is violated, however, legislative and adjudicative procedures are always at hand to restore it, in keeping with that basic principle which is crucial for every institutionally ordered society, namely, the principle of equity, which in this case means appropriate requital: "An eye for an eye and a tooth for a tooth" (5:38).

Equity, however, also exercises a beneficent control over the relationship, the bond, which unites members of the community with one another: "You shall love your neighbor" (5:43). The principle operates when you "love those who love you" and when you "salute . . . your brethren" (5:46,

9

47). For the "neighbor" here is one who belongs to the same group, who reciprocates the "love" with a like sense of belonging. (Compare in this connection the full wording of the text referred to, Lev. 19:18: "You shall not take vengeance or bear any grudge against the sons of your own people, but you shall love your neighbor as yourself . . . .")

Directly related to this matter of inner solidarity is another basic trait which characterizes every group that lives together on a continuing basis: its demarcation from those outside it, the exclusion of nonmembers, who in an extreme case are met with the very opposite of the love that rules within the group, namely, hate: ". . . and hate your enemy" (5:43). A completely open institution is unthinkable.

There is yet another important feature characteristic of life wherever one law holds for all, characteristic, indeed, of every institution as such, namely the subjection of everything to public scrutiny: men practice their piety "before men in order to be seen by them"; they give alms "that they may be praised by men"; "they love to stand and pray in the synagogues and at the street corners, that they may be seen by men"; and they fast "that their fasting may be seen by men" (6:1, 2, 5, 16). Actions that are demanded by generally accepted standards bring to their doer the approval of the other members of the group, and the pursuit of that approval is a strong motive for such actions. In this way the fact of public scrutiny establishes, supports, and gives stability to the social order as a whole and to the actions that go to make it up, of which those cited here — fasting, almsgiving, and praying — are illustrative of many others in the Jewish community.

This positive effect of public approval has as its necessary counterpart a correspondingly public condemnation in cases where someone has been remiss, a "judging" which involves a reciprocal surveillance: "with the judgment you pronounce you will be judged, and the measure you give will be the measure you get" (7:2). This "judgment" and "measure" are not something vague or ill-defined. They are the recognized laws and customs of the community, known to and accepted by every member as the norms for decision and action. Thus the "judging" rests on a solid foundation, and whoever "measures" in these terms has behind him the full authority of the established norms. This "judging," then, this reciprocal surveillance, becomes a firm and indispensable support for the preservation of the social order.

Finally, two other factors are mentioned which are absolute necessities wherever life is to continue on an organized basis: first, the acquisition and maintenance of property, here called "laying up treasures on earth" (6:19); and secondly, work, the deliberate provision for the future, the sowing, toiling, reaping, spinning, the taking thought for "what you shall eat and what you shall drink and what you shall wear" (6:25–31). Without some form of property and of work it is impossible to sustain physical life, the preservation of which is, as we said at the outset, a fundamental concern of every social order.

Thus, in dealing with the norms and behavioral patterns to which it refers under the rubric of "law," the Sermon on the Mount is actually touching on more than simply the Jewish law. It comes to grips with the institutional life of man as such, and in doing so it outlines a permanently valid sketch of what life actually involves: protection of life, preservation of marriage, confirmation of the pledged word, appropriate punishment for any breach of the rules, mutual obligation, exclusion of the outsider, public scrutiny of behavior within the community, reciprocal surveillance, ownership of property, and work as a means of livelihood. All these must be present in some way or other whenever men would live together on any continuing basis.

And when all these factors, so indispensable to the existence of any human institution, were called into question by the repeated assertion, "But I say to you," two things were involved. In the first place, this was a provocative and revolutionary departure into unexplored territory, and its meaning was by no means immediately apparent. In the second place, such radical words at once lifted the debate out of the context of Jewish legalism to a new level of universal significance;

11

they opened up a new question that concerns the people of every era, race, and land, and that goes to the very heart of every social system.

The New Factor: Personal Responsibility

But what could take the place of the "law"? What authority was there, anywhere, that could lay hands on and call into question the indispensable conditions of corporate life? Was not this a highly dangerous game to play? Indeed, from beginning to end the gospel leaves us in no doubt that there *was* being set in motion here a "game" of the utmost gravity and danger. As will be shown later, the Sermon on the Mount repeatedly makes this clear in simple and straightforward language. But what it puts in place of the fixed regulations is set out, point by point, in careful and complete contrast to the rules that characterize institutional life. And if we take all of the individual sayings as a whole, we again find a coherent picture of a pattern of human responsibility, but it is a new kind of pattern.

The new approach made by the Sermon on the Mount is shown most clearly in a section that may well be regarded as its core. Right in the middle are three passages of the same kind, following one hard upon the other, setting out the new attitude in contrast to the old, with respect to alms, prayer, and fasting (6:1–18). It is in these passages, and in those that precede and follow them, that one can see most clearly what is at issue in the contrasts that are set out. The crucial character of this revolution is clearly shown in four aspects.

The first is the downgrading of the institution, the old sacrosanct order of absolute validity. It loses its absolute authority through a step that is simple and yet changes everything: the order itself is questioned with respect to its origins and the source of its validity. And then there appears the countenance of the living, personal God. The last word now is not with the strict morality of almsgiving, prayer, and fasting, but with "your Father who is in heaven" and who "will reward you" (6:1, 4).

Later we shall have to remind ourselves that here the very deepest meaning of the "law" is revealed, namely, that all of the individual commandments proceed from the "I am the Lord your God" (Exod. 20:2). In late Judaism, however, the rigidity of the commandments insinuated itself, separating them from their living Source; and it is with that later rigid form that the Sermon on the Mount comes to grips.

The second aspect of the process is a necessary corollary of the first. As he looks at the actual reality *behind* the rules, the individual himself moves out of their field of force, that is, away from public scrutiny. He is alone now, inaccessible to the control of the institution and removed from its motivating and supportive power. He is addressed as an individual: "Do not let your left hand know what your right hand is doing"; "Go into your room and shut the door and pray to your Father who is in secret"; "Wash your face, that your fasting may not be seen by men" (6:3, 6, 17–18).

The third aspect, however, is that this separate state does not aim at isolation; it does not create an isolated individual, but includes both the person who acts and his opposite number, namely, the recipient when it is a matter of giving, God when it is a matter of praying, and himself when it is a matter of self-discipline (in fasting, to take an obvious example). Clearly, the selection of these three actions is not by chance. In place of one relational grid, that of the established order, there appears a new kind of grid, one which sets man in confrontation with God, with the "neighbor," and with himself, and which requires that he act in and on the basis of this confrontation.

The fourth aspect, then, is that the same action, when removed from the old sphere to the new, completely changes in character; or, to put it more accurately, it now for the first time assumes its own real character. A gift given for the sake of social prestige is no gift, but merely an exchange made on a basis of reciprocity and a balance of services rendered, a basis that is a recognized mark of the institution as such: ". . . they have their reward" (6:2, 5, 16). It is only when that service is not rendered in return that the gift is really a gift. Similarly with prayer: it is genuine conversation with God if, and only if, there is no sidelong glance at the control exercised by public scrutiny. It is only without that control, too, that fasting really becomes self-discipline, whereas previously it was only discipline from without — salutary, to be sure, but of a lesser order.

If we briefly summarize the change that has taken place here, we can say that supervision and guidance, that is, the responsibility for a man's acting aright, has been transferred from one locus to another. Institutional responsibility has changed into responsibility of another kind, which we must call personal, since it arises on a new relational grid where man stands face to face with the person of God, the person of his neighbor, and his own self — which on this grid itself becomes a person. The Sermon on the Mount addresses man no longer primarily as a member of an ordered group, a transient kingdom, but as a citizen of a "kingdom" that is different from, and more than, any human kingdom — as a citizen of the "kingdom of God."

Superficially it seems as if God were simply taking the place of the institution, and that, instead of "having his reward" through public approval, a person receives his reward (or requital) through the "Father who is in heaven" — so that there is apparently a relation between what is given and what is received in exchange, a kind of automatic *quid pro quo* as in the institution.

But that is not so. For the working of an established institution is fixed, limited, public, known inside out and therefore calculable; the expectations one brings to it are of the kind that can be pursued through prosecution at law or achieved through use of force. But such is not the case with God's "reward" or "requital." Anyone who puts his expectations in God, and not in what he can get from the institution, is turning from the limited to the unlimited [*das Offene*], from the fixed to the mobile, from the expected to the unexpected, from calculation to hope, from the known to the new, from that which can be secured by force to that which can only be requested. For God is the "Father" who "knows what you need before you ask him" (6:8). Thus our expectations of him do indeed go into the unlimited [*das Offene*], but not into a vacuum. And so in

14

the sphere of the relationship between God and the individual the same thing may happen as in the public sphere of the institution: motivation, support, response to achievements, judgment of offenses; but it takes place in an entirely new and different way. It is a new and a different kind of responsibility.

Other Features of Personal Responsibility

On the basis of personal responsibility as set out in the crucial section in the Sermon on the Mount, all the other new instructions in the Sermon are built up and set out, point by point, in contrast to institutional responsibility. In one case after another, conduct is freed from the sphere of public control, with its ritual and institutional regulations, and transferred to the sphere of one's personal relationship to God, to one's neighbor as an individual, and to oneself. And in every case this gives the conduct itself a different structure and character.

Thus, we are not to look at the law and judgment that forbid killing, but at the personal relationship to the brother and to the "accuser"; and the ritualistic act of standing before God with a gift at the altar becomes a personal appeal to settle a quarrel. Thus the bald command not to kill is recast into the creation of peace, an act of reconciliation (5:21–26).

The same is true in the section that follows, which deals with the protection of marriage. We are to look beneath the surface of the institution of "marriage" and see the personal relationship in the "heart," and the latter as confronted with God's solemn warning of "hell." Again, the mere abstention from adultery is changed into an active piece of self-discipline. The words that follow, about plucking out one's eye and cutting off one's hand, are blunt and graphic expressions used to make clear that a man's rampant forces must be curbed if he is to be a man, and that he must curb them himself if he is to be a person (5:27–32). The same principle underlies the new understanding of fasting.

Sincere statement, too, is freed from the ritualistic constraint of invoking heaven, earth, the city of Jerusalem, or one's own head. Again we are to look beyond these things to him whose throne is heaven, whose footstool is the earth, whose city is Jerusalem, and who created that head. Before him, the solemn and weighty form of the oath in the presence of witnesses becomes the plain form of speech between one person and the next: "Yes" and "No" (5:33–37).

The complete change of attitude under the new kind of responsibility is especially clear, however, in the instructions that are usually the first to occur to us when the "Sermon on the Mount" is mentioned: refusal to resist evil, and love towards one's enemy. Here personal responsibility pursues a course exactly opposite to that of institutional responsibility (5:39–48).

Whereas in the institution the rule was that of equity, expressed in the requital of evil and in the help given by man to man, the person who is responsible only to God makes himself responsible for everything, renouncing both compensatory retribution and compensatory gift: "But I say to you, Do not resist one who is evil. But if any one strikes you on the right cheek, turn to him the other also . . . . If any one forces you to go one mile, go with him two miles. Give to him who begs from you, and do not refuse him who would borrow from you. . . . For if you love those who love you, what reward have you?" (5:39, 41, 42, 46).

The same renunciation of reciprocity appears later in the repudiation of "judgment," that is, of the reciprocal surveillance that, as has been pointed out, is a powerful and necessary support of any institutional order (7:1–5). In the reciprocal supervision that ruled there, the measuring was always with the same "measure" to which everyone has to submit uniformly. The responsible person's self-control, however, has a different standard, according to which his own fault appears as a "log," and the other person's as a trifling "splinter" in the eye. Everywhere, in requital, in help, and in judgment, there is a similar change: instead of equity and reciprocity we find the individual's unilateral and self-sacrificing acceptance of the burden.

16

There is precisely the same reversal of outlook in one's conduct toward the stranger or one's enemy. The institution excluded and repulsed him. Personal responsibility draws him to itself and builds bridges: "But I say to you, Love your enemies, bless those who curse you, do good to those who hate you, and pray for those who persecute you" (5:44). Through one's "praying" and "blessing," the enemy is placed in the same position before God as is the person himself, whose actions proceed from that position *coram Deo*. For God himself "makes his sun rise on the evil and on the good, and sends rain on the just and on the unjust" (5:45).

Finally, the sections in the Sermon about property and work (6:19–34) represent a very significant change from the old. They concern one's relationship to time, and again there is an essential difference between institutional and personal responsibility. Property ("treasures on earth") provides security for a certain length of time, and so belongs unconditionally to the established order, which, after all, is planned for stability and permanence. We have here, then, a very graphic allusion to the limited duration of property, which is always being threatened by "moth," "rust," "thieves," and many other agents of destruction. Personal responsibility gets its security through quite different "treasures," namely "treasures in heaven," which are not exposed to such assaults. But this means not a still longer period of time, or an absolute indestructability, but duration of quite a different kind, in which time has been left behind altogether.

On the other hand, time is to some extent overcome as an institutional dimension by the Sermon's instructions about work. The institution provides, and must provide, for "tomorrow"; it keeps an eye on the future. It also lives with an ear to the past: "You have heard that it was said to the men of old . . . ." Once more, time is an essential factor. The person, however, lives in the Now: "Therefore do not be anxious about tomorrow, for tomorrow will be anxious for itself. Let the day's own trouble be sufficient for the day" (6:34). The argument for this is in the preceding passage: "Seek first his kingdom

17

and his righteousness, and all these things shall be yours as well." Personal life and personal responsibility find their fulfillment in the ever-new and vital meeting with God, with one's fellowmen, with oneself, and also, no doubt, with things. So, for the person concerned in this meeting, the "Now" is not simply a point of time between past and future, but is also the fulfillment of the present.

So much for the series of contrasts between the two attitudes, which are sharply distinguished by their line of approach and by their structure, and which represent "institutional" and "personal" responsibility.

The Transition from Institutional to Personal

It remains to be made clear the way in which these two types of conduct are related to each other. Throughout the Sermon the method of contrast between the two is a rejection of the one and a summons to adopt the other — the hearer is called on to break away from something old and go forward to something new. It is a matter of a transition.

That leads to the question: What is involved in this transition from the institutional regime to the individual's personal responsibility before God? The text and the context of the Sermon suggest four answers.

1) The transition is a process of secularization, that is, of "making worldly" (*saeculum* = "world"), even if at first glance the opposite seems to be the case. For just because one is continually looking beyond the existing system to the countenance and actions of him who stands behind it, the system itself ceases to be sacrosanct and inviolable; and this simply means that it becomes secularized. The Gospels are full of examples of this from beginning to end — we need only think of the many disputes about the observance of the sabbath.

But the narrow, rigid sanctity that came to light in these disputes had been assimilated by the Jewish law only in the later tradition. According to its wording and general tenor, the law always began its instructions with the creative and vitalizing words: "I am the Lord your God" (Exod. 20:2). And so it can be said in the Sermon on the Mount: "Think not that I have come to abolish the law and the prophets; I have come not to abolish them but to fulfil them" (Matt. 5:17). To "fulfil" means to make the law complete, to give it all the fullness, content, depth, and breadth that was originally intended for it. The Mosaic "law" had itself already pointed beyond a confined ritualistic sanctity, and the prophets had tried to lead their people in the same direction: "I desire steadfast love and not sacrifice, the knowledge of God, rather than burnt offerings" (Hos. 6:6).

2) The transition is a process of personalization. The law is taken out of its rigid reification [*Verdinglichung*], back to the personal God, and is reestablished on that basis. The unconditional *thing* is now to be the unconditional *person*. Man is now to be perfect, not as the law lays down, but "as your heavenly Father is perfect" (Matt. 5:48). That means that man is now addressed as a person and is called on to act responsibly. New powers, hitherto dormant, are awakened, and he is translated into a new status. This status, however, is not that of an isolated individual but of one who stands before God, responds to God, and is answerable to God — answerable, indeed, for his neighbor and for himself. By outlining the individual's relationship to God, to his fellowman, and to himself, the Sermon on the Mount outlines the structure of personal action.

3) The transition is a process of movement, of fluidity. The institution embodies, first and foremost, the principle of tradition, of tenacity, of duration, of unchangeability, as expressed in the formula: "You have heard that it was said to the men of old . . . ." It lays down fixed limits and provides permanent patterns of conduct. The responsible individual, on the other hand, frees himself on principle from any unconditional commitment to these fixed preconditions; he will always make a fresh start through reconciliation, forgiveness, inclusiveness, and giving; and by loving his enemy he obliterates the fixed boundaries. What is numb takes on life, and what is confined breaks out into the open.

4) Finally, the transition is a process toward the perfecting

19

of human existence: "You, therefore, must be perfect, as your heavenly Father is perfect" (5:48). It is concerned with "the way that leads to life" (7:14). Here the Sermon on the Mount agrees with the insights of modern anthropology, which regards man as the being that is "not finally determined." If that is so, it is in the nature of things that anything fixed by the institution fails to touch his real "life." Openness, specifically openness to the world, is fundamental to this living entity with his indeterminate faculties, for whom instincts and environment, "the world of perception and the world of effective action,"[1] do not intermesh to lead toward fixed ends. Every fixation and limitation (and in the case of man, who cannot change his biological equipment, this is bound to be institutional regulation) means a loss to his real life, or an obstacle to its attainment; and the transition from the inflexibility of the institution into open — that is, personal — existence is a "way that leads to life."

At this point we have to look beyond the Sermon itself to the whole context of the gospel in which it stands. It then becomes clear that this "way that leads to life" is meant to be not only a personal process for the individual, but a way for the whole world into a future that is to bring about the full realization of life. In theological terms, the Sermon on the Mount, like the gospel as a whole, must be understood eschatologically. We are to look forward to a goal beyond history, a goal that makes all the history that is still taking place "the last time" and changes its essential character.

The Historical Coexistence of Institution and Person

What has so far been said has not yet enabled us to define adequately the mutual relationship of the two attitudes of institutional and personal responsibility. There remains the unfortunate feeling that we are here shown a way that certainly commands respect, but is nonetheless utopian; and it is with

---

[1] *Merkwelt und Wirkwelt.* See Jakob von Uexküll, "Streifzüge durch die Umwelten von Tieren und Menschen," *Rowohlts Deutsche Enzyklopädie,* Vol. XIII (Berlin, 1934).

this uncomfortable feeling that the Sermon on the Mount has been read again and again all through the history of Christianity. We obviously cannot give up institutional regulations, and the considerations that we have so far set out have actually emphasized the need for them.

In fact, the Sermon does not demand any such renunciation. In the face of every "But I say to you . . ." and every "Do not . . ." with which the institutional structures of life are devalued, there stands clearly and unambiguously at the outset, before the great contrast is made, the statement already quoted, that "the law and the prophets," far from being abolished, are to be "fulfilled." And then we read: "Till heaven and earth pass away, not an iota, not a dot, will pass from the law until all is accomplished" (5:17–19). So the Sermon's meaning and purpose are not the abolition of the institution in favor of a purely personal way of conduct, but their coexistence, their juxtaposition and interpenetration. It is therefore less a question of a transition, as we have called it so far, than an incorporation of something new into what is already there, less a supersession than a completion — in fact, a "fulfillment."

That disposes of any suspicion of an unreal utopia. We must be clear, however, about the mutual relationship of these two coexistent strata. How do these two widely differing attitudes stand, according to the Sermon, within the framework of one and the same historical world? Again we can distinguish certain very different factors.

In the first place, the two are subject to a clear order of precedence: "Seek first his kingdom and his righteousness, and all these things shall be yours as well" (6:33) — "all these things" means all outward security of existence, which is the concern of institutional life. That which is more admirable and vital, more urgent and productive, is personal conduct, the fact of standing within God's field of force, in his "kingdom."

In the second place, it follows directly from the above that personal conduct provides a basis for the institutions, for these are built upon personal responsibility, as we read in the well-known concluding words of the Sermon: "Every one then who

21

hears these words of mine and does them will be like a wise man who built his house upon the rock . . ." (7:24–27).

To this picture of the firm supporting ground are added the two well-known images that do even more justice to the vitality and flexibility of the new order: "You are the salt of the earth" and "You are the light of the world" (5:13, 14) — "you" again means "you who hear these words of mine and do them." The salt does not take the place of food, nor does the light take the place of the house that it illumines; both are additions, but their effect is to stimulate and to open up. They complete, "fulfil," the food and the dwelling; for food without salt is insipid and incomplete, and a building without light is no home.

But in the third place, and in contrast, personal conduct relativizes the institution. It overtops it, forces it open, and takes away its unconditional validity. The consequence of this relativization is that the institution is inevitably hostile to any-one who acts as a free and responsible person; and this is so even if the person is serving the institution. So the Sermon had to contain the prophecy: ". . . men [will] revile you and perse-cute you and utter all kinds of evil against you falsely on my account" (5:11). Jesus himself met his death in the conflict with the sacrosanct Jewish community, and the two thousand years that have passed between his time and ours have re-peatedly — and appallingly — confirmed his prophecy. Time and again the institution claims to be absolute, and will toler-ate no attempt to make it relative. It thinks to gain strength through absoluteness, and does not know that (as the Sermon says) the only institution that stands on the rock is one whose validity is conditional — provided that any curtailment of its authority arises from personal responsibility before God.

The Chances of Realization

There remains one final essential question: What are the chances of realization? Is there any prospect that the new per-sonal life, with its undoubted uncertainty, will be able to pre-vail? The Sermon on the Mount gives two answers: one is gloomy and ends in a cul-de-sac, the other carries us forward; one merely warns, while the other adds to the warning the promise of a bright future. All in all, this is simply what the whole of the New Testament offers to the believer as a future in and beyond history.

The gloomy prediction is that there are certain to be only a few who can go the new way: "The gate is narrow and the way is hard, that leads to life, and those who find it are few" (7:14). The number of those who can endure all the tension, who can live and act in human institutions and at the same time in free responsibility before God, and who can thus be the salt of the earth and the light of the world, will always remain small; the majority are sure to be tied to institutional standards, and will not achieve personal freedom. If only that were all! But behind the gloomy prediction there rises, in fact, a shadowy menace, expressed by the preacher of the Sermon in a strangely melancholy image: "Do not give dogs what is holy; and do not throw your pearls before swine, lest they trample them under foot and turn to attack you" (7:6). Only a few will find the way to personal responsibility, though it is only in doing so that they are justified in regarding the old sacred structures of life as relative and only conditionally valid. But many, and that means many who are unworthy — "dogs" and "swine" — will make a greedy rush for the pearls of the new freedom; they will "trample them underfoot," with the result that the turmoil thus unleashed may also devour those who have spread such dangerous instructions among men. For the instructions are indeed dangerous; they are not merely a solid foundation for building, and the salt of the earth. What was brought into the world here was not only constructive, strengthening, healing force, but dynamite. These words from the Sermon have had appalling corroboration in the course of history, and they are still being corroborated every day. The knowledge of this is reason enough for us to guard ourselves against emasculation or attenuation of the gospel.

Yet this melancholy warning is not the Sermon's last word about the future that it initiates and describes. This "last word" is emphasized through being put in the most conspicuous place in the Sermon, namely, at the beginning, in the beatitudes. They take up the gloomy prediction, but in a new way; and they surmount it: "Blessed are the poor in spirit" (that is, poor in God's living spirit), "for theirs is the kingdom of heaven" (5:3–11). So the danger is not that only a few find the "way to life," the real life of man. The realization of the "kingdom of God," of one's personal being, does not depend on historical success on a broad scale. The very consciousness of a lack of this really effective life leads into God's field of force and into his "blessedness." However, it is, then, not something earned, but a gift; it is a question not of performance and reward, but of that which is freely bestowed. In other words, God's "kingdom," his field of force, is not an institution, but a dimension of personal being; that is evident even from the manner and possibility of its realization.

That is just what is again made clear in the most conclusive way by the last two beatitudes. Just as at the beginning it is a lack of vitality, now it is persecution — again a kind of failure — that is plainly described as a way to the goal. But this persecution occurs, first "for righteousness' sake," and in the next verse "on my account" (5:10, 11). Viewed in the context as a whole, "righteousness" cannot be a mere abstraction, for in that case the personal sphere would be at once undermined by a new legalism. So righteousness emerges here not as an idea, but as a person, as the person who preached the Sermon on the Mount. Personal being here came into the world, not as a doctrine or as an idea, but as an historical person and an historical event, which carried in themselves the whole substance of the matter, and spread their light over the time that followed. If, therefore, we pass in the following pages to the historical consequences of the figure and the event, we are not treading upon new ground. The figure of the preacher from the Mount stands in the center of history; indeed, the Western peoples, in reckoning time, have fixed on his coming as the focal point of history. And that must lead logically to the conclusion that it is also the goal of history.

2

The Middle Ages and the

Present Age in the Light

of the Sermon on the Mount

The Two Sources of Personalization

The development of personal conduct within and beyond its social setting was an historical event; rather, it is a long-term historical process that is still going on. There is ample evidence of this in all branches of historical study: in political, constitutional, social, and economic history, in church history, in the history of law, art, philosophy, and so on. We can see in all of them, in ever-changing perspectives and from different angles, a progressive downgrading of the institution and a corresponding liberation for personal action. But these historical perspectives lead, not merely up to the present time, but right into it and beyond it; and they throw light on the process in which we are still caught up.

The whole development has had two starting points: that of the gospel and, earlier, that of classical Greek civilization, which has also been of the greatest historical significance. Whereas in previous human history outstanding, pioneering individuals had appeared on the scene only rarely, like phenomena of nature — as kings, founders, lawgivers, discoverers, and inventors — it was the Greeks who first really offered to the individual the possibility of acting freely and responsibly. That began in the time of Solon and the tragedians, and the philosophers made a systematic attempt to give it a solid foundation. It is significant that their starting point was, in form, exactly like that of the Sermon on the Mount: they moved away from the traditional order of things by asking what the one permanent factor that underlay it was. Here too the traditional order was relativized, and the thinking individual acquired freedom to criticize, to reform, and to establish new law.

The Greeks' starting point, the ground on which they raised up this new kind of freedom, was that of thought and reason. Its limitations are evident in the work of Plato. His *magnum opus,* the *Republic,* represents a great attempt to advance from this starting point of thought and reason toward a new and serviceable political and social system, in which royal philosophers or philosophical kings would provide their states with new and enduring structures based solely on reason. His own attempts to turn all this into fact so badly disillusioned him, however, that the philosopher, now grown old, in resignation wrote the great work of his late years, the *Laws,* in which he returned to the old structures, deliberately restoring them as sacrosanct, in a compromise between tradition and reason. In Greek philosophy, man as an individual got so far as to see himself as a thinker and a rational being. Therein lay his greatness, but also his limitation.

On the other side of that boundary something more profound lay obscured. We see this from the fact that in the classical and the succeeding Hellenistic periods there was only a progressive disintegration of the old traditional structures, a dissolution of their rootage in their native soil, and a congeries of isolated and detached structures. In the Hellenistic Mediterranean world no new pattern of social structures was created on any large or permanent scale to replace the old; no new world of social orders arose out of the atrophy and disintegration of the traditional sacrosanct bonds of the Mediterranean world. So there came about the final dissolution of classical antiquity, as Plato in his old age had foreseen with penetrating insight to be inevitable: a structure of "laws" with an artificial tradition and an artificial sanctity descended on an unstable world and gave it once again a stature and stability that lasted for centuries; the Roman Empire took over the forms and traditions of the ancient world, but the individualism to which it gave play was circumscribed and did not form the basis of any new development.

At that very moment of history, however, when this final dissolution of antiquity was taking place under Caesar Augustus, there originated in an outlying part of the Roman Empire the second point of departure toward the overcoming of the sacrosanct institution. It was a movement that at first had hardly any contact with the other, that is, with Hellenism and philosophy. This second starting point now made its way across the boundary where the first had been halted; it consisted, as we have seen, of the gospel and the liberation of the person. It was able to cross the boundary because here, in contrast to Hellenism, the historical man did not press forward by his own strength; rather, he experienced in faith the self-revelation of that one last permanent factor, round which the thought of the Greeks had revolved, and which was now revealed as the living God and the Son of God in flesh and blood. In his word man heard the call and challenge to be a person himself.

This new starting point, which in its calculation of time posterity has designated as the real and decisive breakthrough, now penetrated into the fermenting postclassical world that was spanned by the Roman Empire; there it soon came into contact with the other point of departure, namely, the philosophic thought initiated by the Greeks, and became intimately allied with it. Among the great figures responsible for the development of this process we may mention Origen. The two movements combined to produce a new and profound kind of personal existence, thought, and action. And during the next two thousand years this new, profoundly personal existence showed that it possessed the fecundity, the native strength, to create social structures of a new and personal kind which had eluded late Greek antiquity, notwithstanding the latter's high level of intellectual achievement. It was here that the seed of a new world was sown, our modern world, which took over and assimilated the legacies of all the preceding epochs of Mediterranean and Near Eastern history, but completely refashioned them.

The living structure within which this reshaping was begun and set on its course was the Christian church, in whose lap the modern world was nursed in infancy, although the modern world is hardly aware of the fact. The formation of the "community" under the gospel — that also means under the Sermon on the Mount — meant a completely fresh start in the social history of mankind. From the very beginning this community penetrated the traditional social institutions, such as family and state, or incorporated them into itself, and thus transformed them into something new. It was an immense, many-sided, and protracted process of reform and reconstruction; here we can indicate only a very few of the factors that are important for our purpose.

So it was that, as the era of classical antiquity was ending, the Christian church became the bipolar structure that is delineated in the Sermon on the Mount: it made life revolve round the two focal points, the institution and the individual responsible to God. This is developed most clearly and effectively in the figure and writings of Augustine, the two poles being most clearly described in his two best-known and most important works, the *Confessions* and the *City of God*. In the *Confessions* Augustine has given us an account of his personal development more intimate and comprehensive than that of any previous writer in antiquity. The following is the judgment of an authority: "It is true that 'Know thyself' had long been written on the walls of the temple at Delphi, and that from Heraclitus to Tertullian classical and Christian thought had repeatedly pressed forward into the secret places of the mind; but through his passionate self-portrayal Augustine sur-

passed all his predecessors. His portrayal was no longer classical, it was Christian . . . . He descends into the *grande pro-
fundum homo,* into the abyss of man, and in exposing all his
alleys, recesses, hiding places, Augustine speaks to himself, for
himself, and for all mankind, of what he experienced there."[1]

In the other work, the *City of God,* Augustine speeds the
young church on its way with its Magna Carta: "It is itself the
City of God, and again it is not."[2] Here is expressed the tension
involved where the person who is responsible to God treats the
institution as something that is only relative: "In the 'City of
Worldliness' such things as body and pleasure, family and
property, work and the state, art and science, are absolute; in
the 'City of God' they are relative . . . . Everything that the
latter is willing to allow as belonging by nature or in its own
right to the good things of civilization, even the basic structures
of social life, savors of compromise. Social units, and in particular the state, are valued according as they raise or lower the
personality of the individual."[3]

The church, regarding itself in the light of Augustine's City
of God, completely vanquished and supplanted two religious
worlds: (1) the mixture of what was left of the ancient cults
and mystery religions in the Mediterranean region, which were
overarched by the sacral aura of imperial Rome; and (2) the
nature religions of the Celts, Teutons, and Slavs, pressing in
from the North. One thing was neither vanquished nor supplanted: the sacred edifice out of which, and in opposition to
which, the gospel itself had arisen, the Jewish religion of the
law, on which even to this day the gospel has made no serious
inroads. But the syncretism of late antiquity, although be-
queathing a rich inheritance, succumbed to the church; and
the younger primitive peoples, now developing into nations
with their own history, soon thereafter, if not quite simultaneously, also accepted Christianity and became its new and
doughty standard-bearers.

[1] Joseph Bernhart, *Augustinus* (Stuttgart, 1947), pp. 14–15.
[2] *Ibid.,* p. 26.
[3] *Ibid.,* p. 25.

Institution and Person in the Middle Ages

It can come as no surprise that both the church, revolving round the two focal points of institution and person, and the monarchical states and smaller social units that grew up in that general setting were again shaped at first predominantly on institutional lines and less by the personal factor. The Mediterranean region had grown accustomed to the supporting scaffolding of the political system imposed by Rome; the emperor Constantine had by law united the Christian church with that system, and all the emerging peoples were still organized along collective lines rather than in individual units. Among the Germans, tribal ties were of basic importance also for the later structures of the feudal system and the brotherhood.[4] Wilhelm Grönbech says of these tribal relationships that "the individual's action means that all are acting in and with him; one individual cannot suffer without involving the whole circle. So absolute is the connection that the individual as such cannot exist at all; as soon as the bond is weakened he sinks down, the most wretched of all creatures."[5] Such pristine institutional ties could not be severed with one blow. Consequently in the Middle Ages there took shape, on Celtic and Slavic as well as on Roman and Germanic foundations, a new world of predominantly traditional and sacrosanct orders — in church and empire, village and feudal estate, parish and monastery, guild and municipality. Concern for the "individual soul" was not lacking, but it did not dominate the social pattern. The whole of life was permeated above all by "Christian morality," which was decidedly a power of the institutional kind.

In looking back, we like to think of the Middle Ages as the really Christian world. Yet the medieval order of things was dominated by what the Sermon on the Mount calls the "law"; it was the institution, not the person, that held the field. As evidence of this, a few illustrations must suffice.

---

[4] [*Genossenschaft,* an association formed to further the members' common interests, usually economic. — TRANS.]

[5] Wilhelm Grönbech, *Kultur und Religion der Germanen* (5th ed.; Stuttgart: W. Kohlhammer-Verlag, n.d.), I, 40–41.

The social structures were designed to conform basically to the principles of permanence, stability, and tradition, in accord with the "good old law" that Fritz Kern has described as the principle of medieval law and constitution in the Middle Ages; this was a holy ordering, and whoever violated it was offending against God and the law. "The law was considered part of the cosmic system, and therefore unshakable."[6] And, in fact, many regulations lasted not only throughout the Middle Ages, but also through succeeding centuries. In the papacy, in monasticism, in the empire that harked back to Charlemagne, in the communities of the mark system,[7] the guiding principle was, in effect, "You have heard that it was said to the men of old . . . ."

Consequently, as the regulations were, in their legal conception, sacrosanct, their whole existence was bound up with the altar. From its inception the empire was a "Holy Empire," even though it did not assume that name till the time of Frederick Barbarossa. Towns had their own patron saints; the guilds had grown out of religious fraternities and retained a religious character; the village assembled in its own church. With a solemn oath one bound oneself to one's lord, to the federation of brotherhoods, or to the citizenry. The oath also gave a legal basis to feudal authority and voluntary association.

Moreover, these social structures were of an institutional nature, whose "law" was observed even in the minutest details of daily life. Customs and morals, common law and statute law, religious belief, one's dialect, dress, or craft — all were mingled in indissoluble union. As established characteristics of one's station in life, they embodied the "expectation that life would be lived in a specific way."[8]

In these things, too, there was unrestricted public scrutiny.

[6] Fritz Kern, *Recht und Verfassung im Mittelalter* (2d ed.; Darmstadt: Wissenschaftliche Buchgesellschaft, 1958), p. 13.
[7] [A designation of the medieval system of common ownership and cultivation of tracts of land by groups of freemen, who also governed their own communities, called "marks," probably after "mark" in the sense of boundary. — TRANS.]
[8] Max Weber, *Wirtschaft und Gesellschaft* (*Grundriss der Sozialökonomik*, Part 3 [Tübingen, 1922]), p. 635.

31

It was not till a later period that the phenomenon of "private life" appeared on the scene. In town and village, market and monastery, everyone's life was open for all to see, and was requited, or tolerated, or upheld, with praise or blame, approval or disapproval.

In such public scrutiny it was not only possible, but expected, that one person should pass judgment on the other. Church discipline and professional honor presupposed that kind of watchful and continuous reciprocal surveillance and also provided fixed standards of undoubted authority for that judgment. Thus the individual was taken firmly in hand from without, through the institution, and insofar as that was so, he was relieved of the duty of self-discipline. The ethical standard was primarily and principally the institutional standard.

Any violation of person, property, or honor was dealt with on the basis of requital. The feud was not of itself a breach of the law, but a "fundamental element in every medieval constitution";[9] and, depending on one's station in life, both the knightly duel and the peasants' tussles continued to be obligatory long after the Middle Ages.

Brotherly love was considered to be due in the first place to those of the same brotherhood or feudal estate, with the principles of "peace" and "loyalty" being understood to entail strict reciprocity of obligations and services.[10]

It was in line with all this that outsiders were treated as such. The exclusiveness, and even hostility, between classes, villages, towns, and families was apt to degenerate into permanent rancor, which we who live in later times are apt to think of as "medieval."

These examples must suffice. They are enough to show that, despite its designation as "Christian," this traditional and sacrosanct system inclined more toward the "law" than toward what the Sermon on the Mount describes as the "kingdom of heaven" with its obligation of personal responsibility. Of course, we

[9] Otto Brunner, *Land und Herrschaft. Grundfragen der territorialen Verfassungsgeschichte Südostdeutschlands im Mittelalter* (Munich, 1943), p. 23.
[10] *Ibid.*, p. 120.

must not paint a wholly lopsided picture. The medieval social structures were also characterized by certain features that gave, or at least could give, more scope for individual freedom than had been the case with the sacrosanct orders of pre-Christian times. There was, for instance, the division of power into spiritual and secular, which in the area dominated by Rome did not culminate in an undivided and all-powerful authority, as happened in the Eastern Byzantine caesaropapism. One might also mention the formation of brotherhoods, which helped to prevent domination by the nobility and thereby enlarged and safeguarded the sphere of freedom. Preeminent in this stratified society, however, was the system of strict regulation under which anyone who tried to go his own way was a marked man, and which thus made his existence a hazardous one.

Institution and Person Today

So much for the surprising results attained when we use the yardstick of the Sermon on the Mount, and therefore of the gospel itself, to measure the medieval order of things, which was closely bound up with the church in an age of cathedrals, monasteries, and institutions of mercy, Christian chivalry, and crusades with their holy zeal. It is just as well that we should cut the ground from under a Christian romanticism, a regretful ecclesiastical backward glance from our unecclesiastical world to a supposedly golden age ordered on Christian principles.

This view is demolished further if we measure our present circumstances by the same yardstick. Indeed, the result may be even more surprising. If we look for once not at what present-day existence *is,* but at the *demands* that it makes on us by reason of its structure, we shall see that it goes a surprisingly long way toward meeting the commands of the Sermon on the Mount with respect to personal responsibility. There is a striking correspondence between the kind of responsibility outlined there and the attitude that the person of the twentieth century must adopt if he is to be equal to the situations with which our century confronts him.

Thus the dominant characteristic of our time is not tradition but movement. Durability and stability have receded far into the background. According to our conception of law, new law necessarily supersedes old law; in the early and middle periods of the Middle Ages it was the other way round. And none of our secular institutions is surrounded any longer by a halo of sanctity. The scene is dominated by reorganization, restructuring, the liquidation of businesses, associations, and unions, and the dissolution of institutions and even of states. "We are compelled by circumstances . . ." is a stronger argument than "You have heard that it was said to the men of old . . . ." Even property is no longer any lasting guarantee for the future; and although, thanks to technical progress, we are better protected today than formerly against moth and rust, we now have currency devaluations, bombings, agrarian reforms, expropriations, bankruptcies, and so on. These things have compelled us to heed the words "Do not be anxious about tomorrow" and have often made us realize that tomorrow will indeed "be anxious for itself." All this presents a remarkable and glaring contrast to the incessant small- and large-scale planning of our time, but it is true all the same.

Present-day "law," too, is characterized by flexibility and jurisdictional restrictions, in spite of, or indeed because of, the immense and continuous production of laws, in which card index files have replaced stone or bronze tablets. In business transactions, for instance, the only thing that is now strictly binding, apart from some residual customs, is the "law" in the restricted sense of the laws and statutes of the state. The force of custom, which in the Middle Ages was not, or was not clearly, separated from law, is no longer strictly binding. So in the legal sense the law has come to be a broader framework for our day-to-day affairs, leaving our actual conduct plenty of free play. Without breaking out of that framework, one can act by the most varied ethical standards, ranging from the most contemptible to the most upright. And when, in order to be formally correct, we observe the social amenities, these are mainly practical and have little ethical significance. In short,

34

the norm is no longer to be relied on; and this at a time when we are being swamped with norms and prescriptions as never before.

Moreover, public scrutiny has today become limited and quite uncertain in its action. There are two reasons for this. First, all institutional life outside the family has become organized life; that means that the individual in his work or other activity open to public view always shows a part, and not the whole, of his personality. Public scrutiny therefore never sees and judges one's whole character or the whole situation, and so its judgment must necessarily be open to question. Secondly, this mobile and fragmented organized life lacks, as we have already said, norms of conduct that are stable, well-tried, and generally known and acknowledged; and that means, again, that public scrutiny provides an unreliable judgment without the necessary ethical guidance and responsibility. The individual therefore, set free by a faulty public scrutiny and by the fragmentation of organized life really to be an individual, withdraws, so far as that is possible, into the realm of privacy and the incognito of the crowd. This, too, is in remarkable contrast to what one might at first suppose of a time that has unprecedented means of public scrutiny at its disposal. We might suppose that newspaper, radio, and television, which have made it possible to survey the whole world, have created a means of public scrutiny much more effective than that of earlier periods. But news bulletins alone do not create a public scrutiny.

It is only another way of expressing the same thing if we say that today it is no longer possible for one person meaningfully to "judge" another, that is, to undertake responsibility for keeping his conduct under surveillance, as was possible, usual, and salutary in previous generations. In fact, judging was one of the functions of public scrutiny, and along with the latter, and for the same reasons, it has lost its certainty and justification. Passing judgment on someone else is now generally a matter of subjective opinion that imposes no obligations, and the person in question repudiates the judgment, often not without reason, as false and offensive. And even if the judgment hits home, it may be met with the retort: "Mind your own business; I know what I'm doing." Today, mutual criticism does not help to sustain corporate life, as it used to; on the contrary, it poisons it.

Thus, in our day man is thrown back on self-criticism, and he claims the right to practice it. And if this kind of criticism is the most stringent of all, it is even more so at a time when all standards have become shaky. But these standards from the past were preeminently institutional, and such standards are inadequate for self-criticism. For self-criticism is a personal achievement and, as we know from the Sermon on the Mount, is structurally quite different from institutional controls, and measures with standards different from those of the institution. Our own age is therefore confronted with the task of deliberately creating and using the standards of personal self-criticism.

But we may go further. The possibility of meaningful requital has today reached its limits. The state long ago abolished the right to participate in an armed feud or duel, and reserved to itself the sole right to the use of force: on the domestic scene, in the form of police measures, the administration of justice, and the imposition of punishment; abroad, in the form of war. For a long time these governmental methods for the use of force were employed in a meaningful way in the sense of institutional requital; and the result was a large measure of stability, both domestic and international. But in the recent decades of revolutions and world wars, of the widespread misuse of force by the state, of concentration camps, prisoner of war camps, and internment camps, of bombings and large-scale displacement of peoples, of rigged political trials and perversions of justice, the world has been invaded by an unlimited flood of violence which can no longer be disguised as requital. So far, any retribution for acts of violence committed in our time has simply meant a further delay in the advent of peace. There can be no way out of this situation except through forgiveness.

It is equally clear that in the changed conditions there is no sense whatever in any absolute hostility. For today, in contrast to the socially stratified world of another day, we do not have rigidly demarcated groups of people. This too is because the principle of organization has taken over so completely; since only a part of one's personality is engaged in a particular place, all alike are placed in an immense, intricately interwoven net. All are involved together, and an endless chain of causes and effects is operative all over the world. Unlimited enmities, such as might exist in peasants' quarrels and family feuds, crusades and wars against the Turks, are now suicidal. It was through national hatreds and ideological crusades that our former political world came to grief. Today the situation itself, in small matters as well as great, compels us to move toward reconciliation with the enemy, since we are all in the same boat. It is necessary to recall this in a world that is rent by deadly hostilities and seems to have forgotten the art of peacemaking.

Nor can we rely any longer on reciprocity of service, loving only those who love us. Our highly mobile world is continually taking us into situations where we have to establish new relationships with strangers, and this is always apt to mean giving something in advance without being sure of repayment. Indeed, in many instances it means rendering a service with no possibility whatever of repayment; that is always the case when people who meet us only briefly and in passing are forced by circumstances to depend on us, and in some way or other are entrusted to our responsibility. That, too, is a strange but undoubted fact of experience at a time when everything seems to have become commercialized, with nothing to be had except on payment.

If we now try to sum up what we have been saying, we arrive at a strange conclusion. In the light of the Sermon on the Mount, we can see our own age from an entirely new angle. The things that we have mentioned are unpleasantly familiar to us: blueprints without regard to people; the continuous flood of new laws and regulations; the excessive opportunities for journalistic inquiries into the most intimate recesses of private life and for broadcasting their results; the shattering of all ethical standards; the deadly vortex of violent retaliation and counterretaliation; the absence of peace in a world rent by stresses and hatreds; the universal commercialization of life, with the first question asked always being that of payment. All this is well known to everyday experience, and vigilant critics of modern culture never tire of pointing to new aspects of these evils and distresses. But we are now in a position to see that all such conclusions remain on the periphery, and that at the heart of these externals there is a center, a hidden center, on which everything must necessarily converge: a quite specific form of responsibility, which approaches, point for point, the kind of responsibility indicated in the Sermon on the Mount. It is always open to that which is new, and it is flexible enough to change. It knows that all material security is provisional and uncertain. It does not blindly follow external standards, and it turns from an inchoate and largely irresponsible public scrutiny to make its own decisions in its own way. It relies, not on the external surveillance exercised by the attitude of the crowd, but on self-criticism based on standards of a new kind. It believes that only by forgiving even the most terrible crimes can it break the chain of atrocities. It has a thousand threads to connect it even with the enemy, and it always feels ultimately responsible for other people with whom there is not yet, and perhaps cannot be, any reciprocity of service.

Preliminary Conclusions

The demands made on us by our own time are remarkably like those made on us by the Sermon on the Mount. The idea that the "Christian" Middle Ages were further than our own perplexed, secularized, and skeptical age from the real content of the gospel sounds too strange to be accepted on the spot. For we are too accustomed to regard the transition to our own time, from a spiritual point of view, as a kind of backsliding from Christianity.

On the other hand, when we look at this resemblance aright, we find it so significant that we have to go further in the direction that it suggests; and in doing so, we find that it leads us to a number of very important conclusions.

There is first the general conclusion that, if we are to master our world, it will be not along institutional lines or by institutional methods but primarily and especially through the person. We can no longer base our hopes on a system of regulations or on our awareness of such a system; on the contrary, we may expect pacification, reconciliation, and unity, if at all, only by virtue of the person. That means that we must seek a cure for our ills in an entirely different direction, since our own age has been trying to find its salvation by perfecting our social institutions and by planning our social system in ever-greater detail.

The conclusions are significant, too, for the relationship of the Christian message to modern society. Of course, this message will, on the one hand, always confront modern society, as it has every past society, as the "wholly other," judging it, setting limits to it, and relativizing it. On the other hand, an inner relationship between the two will become discernible, a mutual regard and convergence that cannot fail to make their mark on the message and life of both church and society. For the church can be greatly strengthened by this hidden alliance, both in its message and in its patterns of life. And modern society, still seeking to understand itself, can receive in this way helpful interpretations of its presuppositions, its bases, and its opportunities for the future, and so can be materially helped to achieve clarity regarding its own nature. In other words, there emerges once again the relationship, at once challenging and creative, which we have already seen in the Sermon itself, and which is fundamental to the gospel in contrast to all other patterns of life as we know them from history. But in every epoch the church must strive anew to achieve the particular relationship which at that particular time will both challenge and establish the existing society, for the aloofness of church and society, as well as their mutual attraction, can assume very diverse forms.

The nature of that inner relationship in our modern society, however, is undoubtedly conditioned by history. So, before we look in detail at society as it is at present constituted, we shall have to take a backward glance at its development. This backward glance, moreover, will make it even more evident that our time is one of transition.

Part II

The Organization

3

The Evolution of

the Organization

What Is an Organization?

In the previous chapter the world of "the Middle Ages" (the term is a decided oversimplification) was compared with the modern world in the light of the Sermon on the Mount. We saw that the medieval period was dominated by a kind of institution that was stable, rooted in tradition, and oriented toward the altar. Despite a number of distinctive characteristics, which could be indicated only briefly and partially, and which were seen to be Christian in origin, the period presented us with established orders—hallowed institutions such as had existed in pre-Christian times and places, or still exist in non-Christian regions. We said, therefore, that, in general, these orders were to be designated by what the Sermon refers to as "law." In the modern world, however, as we have seen, something different has emerged. There are now no orders and institutions — or hardly any — whose validity is hallowed, unconditional, and dictated by tradition. Our lives are no longer shaped by a vast sacrosanct framework of orders and institutions; our age is characterized instead by change and by social structures of only conditional validity. That, of course, does not mean that we have ceased to have social structures; it simply means that we now have structures of a different kind. Our institutions are no longer sacrosanct and traditional, but are built up on a different principle, which we call — using the widely accepted term — the *principle of organization*. Life today is structured almost wholly along organizational lines. These organizations do indeed provide us with support, but not always with complete stability: they are always subject to reshaping or "reorganization." Whether we can understand our own age will depend largely on whether we rightly understand the phenomenon of the organization.

To understand the nature of an organization we may first refer to the characteristics that emerged when we looked briefly at our own age in the light of the Sermon on the Mount. The distinguishing marks of a particular age are also the distinguishing marks of the prevailing institutional pattern. And here once again we find that our point of departure in the gospel and the Sermon provides enlightenment, for it helps us to grasp not just random features, but the really characteristic ones.

The organization itself is a flexible structural pattern, in contrast to the traditional world ordered along stratified and sacrosanct lines, a world that was concerned with long-term stability, even in minute details. Social structures based on organization always remain subject — at least in theory — to necessary changes. A business, a federation, a cooperative, can be reorganized at any time if competitive conditions change, if there are technical innovations, or if new demands by the public have to be met. With changing situations, changing problems, and changing methods of work the organization must change too, if it is not to stagnate and become unproductive. It stays alive by remaining alert and flexible; that is one of its basic attributes. Of course, it has traditions too, but they can be given only limited play, and they always have to be carefully watched.

That suggests, in the second place, a certain relation to time, a relation different from that of the traditional institutions. It is undoubtedly true that an organization has its origins in the past: at the beginning it was pointed in a certain direction; a great deal of experience has been accumulated through hard work; and, from the financial standpoint, the capital with which it works is always, in the last analysis, the fruit of past work, even if it was first raised in the form of credit. But if the organization has any vigor, it is much more influenced by the future. Future production, concern for the future representation of its interests, future arrangements for product distribution, must of necessity determine the shape and scale of the business organization, the mechanism of the corporation. The correct forecasting of future demands or of marketing opportunities, the correct planning in advance for the necessary labor and machinery, in short, foresight and not hindsight — these are the mainspring of the organization. It draws its life from the future more than from the past.

In the third place, our organizations are, as we said earlier, completely secularized. No method of work, no demarcation of authority, no chain of command, and no form of cooperation is sacred and inviolable. Employment in a business or member-ship in a federation is settled simply by contract or written statement, and no longer with the oath or pledge with which, in the Middle Ages, one entered the service of a master or joined a brotherhood. For that reason, work patterns and other organizational patterns, as well as membership in the organization, can be flexible and amenable to change, as best suits the changing conditions. In our day a taboo on change would very soon lead to stagnation.

In the fourth place, the power of the organization is only conditional and limited; it is valid relatively, and not abso-lutely. This again is an unfailing characteristic of modern so-cial structures, and it represents an important contrast with the old stratified feudal structures and those of the medieval brotherhoods. This limitation consists in a restriction of aims. It is often asserted that the decisive mark of an organization is its pursuit of a purpose. That is not quite accurate. The me-dieval manorial system, the peasants' communities of the thousand-year-long mark system, and the craft guilds were purposeful — and in fact intelligently purposeful. The difference is rather that those old traditional institutions pursued a multiplicity of aims — political, economic, legal, ecclesiastical, social, ethical — so that it was extremely difficult, if not impossible, to determine precisely the limits of their authority. A modern organization, on the other hand, such as a business firm or an association of people with common interests, may well pursue several aims, but the scope of those aims cannot be extended at will; there is no going beyond a limited radius. And the organization's power is limited by this restriction of its aims; it can function properly only insofar as, and only in those areas where, its proper aims are adhered to. To that extent its power is limited.

Now, this limited power of the organization points to a final characteristic, which is perhaps the most important of all, and in which all those previously mentioned converge: it is essentially the business of the organization to allow its members freedom of action. To express it differently: the members of an organization are more than just members; the whole range of their existence is not simply their employment by this or that business, or their membership in this or that association. That is already evident formally, from the fact that today it is usual, and in fact often necessary, to belong to several or even a large number of organizations at once. In the Middle Ages, on the other hand, one could belong to only one "household," and at the same time to only one guild or corporation. Membership in more than one such body was exceptional, and was frowned on.

The reasons for the freedom that finds its outward expression in this way lie at the heart of the matter. They will have to be discussed frequently in the following pages, for we are touching here on the real subject, the real thesis, of this whole book. The question of personal freedom is, after all, central to all the open or smoldering social conflicts of the present time. And if up to this point we have been speaking of personal responsibility we can now add personal freedom, for both mean the same. What is at issue is liberation for personal responsibility.

This setting free within the organization is rooted in the new relationship to the facts of the case [*Sache*]. For even if methods of work, organizational patterns, and procedures are open, flexible, and changeable, it does not mean that they are left up in the air and subject to arbitrary caprice. It is simply that tradition has been replaced by another yardstick, a new means of discipline, namely the relationship to the facts of the case. We take that term to mean the overall structure, open to change and not subject to rigid demarcation, and including purpose, resources, and other considerations that may help or hinder. It is all-important that the organization should correspond as nearly as possible with these facts as they exist at any particular time. To ensure this, however, there must be men in the organization who are as free as possible to adopt this objective [*sachliche*] attitude, and whose actions are not cramped by hidebound regulations. Such freedom can be the prerogative of one person in the organization, or of several, or of all; and it can be given in varying measure to different people according to their responsibilities. In the case of a textile factory, for instance, an individual or an executive board, together with a board of directors, has the responsibility and the freedom of decision for the whole. In addition, within the company there are departmental managers and foremen with a certain amount of discretionary power, but even the individual workman or employee will have a larger or smaller measure of freedom to arrive at appropriate [*sachliche*] solutions to the problems of his own job. In all organizations every individual member will cooperate even in the making of decisions for the whole body by means of voting and election of the leadership.

This new kind of relation to the facts of the case within the organization has been taken into account from the outset by the development of a new and more independent attitude toward the organization. In the Middle Ages, entry into one of the institutions of the time was by means of a contract, which has been called a "status contract."[1] Here, it is true, the relationship could be terminated, but as long as it stood it bound

---

[1] *Statusvertrag.* See Carl Schmitt, *Verfassungslehre* (Berlin: Duncker & Humblot, 1954).

the whole man in every aspect of his personality; the contract involved a comprehensive reciprocal obligation. The development of the new principle of organization brought in its place the "free contract" between individuals, which establishes individual relationships whose content is essentially subject to certain defined limits. The same is true of membership in a club or society, where the newcomer assumes certain delimited rights and duties. In no case, therefore, does joining an organization involve the whole of a man's personality. He is not identified wholly, and without residue, with the organization.

In the Western countries, where the organization has been developed most consistently and over the longest period of time, the development has been carried a step further. The person who, as required by the facts of the case, must be free both within and toward organizations has also been left free to choose whether he will join an organization at all, which one he will join, and how long he will stay in it. Freedom of association and freedom to choose one's occupation and place of work have long been an essential part of all liberal constitutions. They are included in the basic law of many lands. There is no doubt, not only that these added freedoms are desirable, but also that they follow with compelling logic from the nature of the organization and are vital to its complete development.

If we recapitulate the features that together characterize the organization as it has developed, we again see a combination that is now familiar, but nonetheless surprising: the modern organization, in contrast to the older traditional and sacrosanct orders and institutions, is marked by flexibility, secularization, limited authority, and personal responsibility. These changes are similar to those made in the old "law," with its rigid ritualism, by the Sermon on the Mount, as we saw in comparing them point by point. This reinforces and deepens our impression of the remarkable insight that we first saw exhibited in our own age as a whole. If we came to see that the structure of our undoubtedly very "unchristian" age points in the direction of the gospel much more than do the "Christian Middle Ages," we now see the same thing again in the underlying social structure of this age, the organization. Surprisingly, it differs from the old sacrosanct orders and institutions in the very direction indicated by the gospel itself. This prompts the thought that the gospel was the motive force that produced the change. We shall now take a look at this development.

The Main Turning Points in the Evolution of the Organization

It is not possible, within the scope of this book, to relate even in its outlines the history of the very tortuous route along which the modern structural pattern of the organization has evolved out of the earlier sacrosanct world of tradition, nor is it necessary to do so in our present context. All that need be done here is to point out a few decisive turning points that helped increasingly to give the current its new course, and made it deeper, wider, and stronger. We shall see that the Christian faith not only influenced those particular events, but was their main cause. We are indebted to Eugen Rosenstock-Huessy for pointing out the first of these turning points. In his well-known book on revolutions, a work filled with penetrating insights and illuminating connections of diverse materials, he names the "papal revolution" of Gregory VII as the beginning of the history of the revolutions in Europe and elsewhere.[2] It is a surprising thought that the embryo of all the great world-shaking revolutions should originate within the oldest and most conservative of all European institutions; but such is indeed the case. And Rosenstock-Huessy himself hints at something else that must be added for our purposes: these great movements brought with them their own new social structure — the organization.

As the document that marks the breakthrough of the organization, Rosenstock-Huessy cites the *Dictatus Papae,* the programmatical writing of the great reformer pope Gregory VII. Composed in 1075, but kept secret at first, it was subsequently implemented point for point by Gregory's successors.

[2] Eugen Rosenstock-Huessy, *Out of Revolution: Autobiography of Western Man* (New York: William Morrow & Co., 1938), pp. 537 ff.

It is here that we actually find the decisive formula that meant the abandonment of the sacred and therefore supposedly unchangeable order of things. Among other things, the pope claimed the right to "make new laws as circumstances required." This was really revolutionary. We are today so used to this principle that it is difficult to realize how shocking and earthshaking this claim must have seemed in a world that regarded the "good old law" as a sacred prescriptive right and was capable of understanding legal renovations only as the restoration of old laws that had become obscured. This was indeed a revolution, and if we do not regard the event too much as an isolated occurrence, we can see that here began a movement which, at times slowly and covertly, at other times in violent eruptions visible from afar, transformed the situation in Europe and in the world.

This escape from the traditional institution into a more spacious dimension, where it was possible to be free to introduce changes in that institution as demanded by the facts at hand and the requirements of the situation, was the act of an individual. To be sure, not an individual like the great kings and founders and pioneers of former times, but one who claimed for himself and his successors the perpetual right to do this by virtue of the office he occupied. Thus freedom from the institution was taken into the institution itself. But that is precisely the relationship of tension that was disclosed in the Sermon on the Mount, and it is also the most significant characteristic of the organization. In a conflict that shook the world — one need only think of Gregory's struggle with the emperor Henry IV and the latter's journey to Canossa — one impassioned individual achieved the freedom of personal existence *within* the institution and yet *above* it.

What emerged here, however, was not simply the personal fervor of a man called Gregory, formerly a monk named Hildebrand. This was the fulfillment of a thousand years' heritage, which had worked ceaselessly to unite the Greek philosophical conception of the individual with the Christian conception of personal existence *coram Deo*. There now began another thousand years, during which this idea of personal existence was to reshape the world.

Gregory himself began that reshaping forthwith, and his successors developed it to an amazing extent. For the new freedom at the church's summit necessarily affected the whole edifice: it was turned into an "organization." There arose here, in the form of the ecclesiastical hierarchy, the first organization of western Europe and of the world. From the pope, at the top, downward, all the ranks (including those previously existing) of metropolitans, bishops, and lower church orders, were changed into a disciplined pyramid of officeholders oriented upward. This meant that all of these subordinate offices were also placed under the principle of a flexibility informed by the facts at hand, with the result that the principle was widely disseminated. There now came into being the official bodies of the curia, which apportioned the power at the summit into areas of responsibility for specific tasks. The freedom to make new laws that was claimed, and exercised, was reflected in the *Corpus Juris Canonici,* which expanded steadily under the discretionary authority of papal decisions. These formed western Christendom's first legal code in which old law was superseded by new; hitherto it had been the other way round — at least in conception, and according to legal theory.

Prior to this the world had known rigid hierarchies of officials — in the Egyptian kingdom, in the Roman Empire, or in Byzantium, which through the centuries claimed to be the legitimate successor of Rome. But in the Roman clergy of the high Middle Ages this ancient structure was modified by the addition of an entirely new element that made for movement and change. It was still very restrained, and held in check by tradition; nonetheless, as Rosenstock-Huessy has shown, it was the germ of a radical, world-shaking revolution. That element was the free person before God, the person for whom the existing order was only conditionally valid and could, and indeed must, be changed "as circumstances required." At first it was only one individual who claimed the explosive force of this freedom, on behalf of all others, feeling that he was upheld and supported by his high office as the representative of Christ and the successor of the apostles.

Proceeding from its original, basic form, this new structure, the "organization," was disseminated afar in the succeeding centuries, slowly at first, and then more rapidly as time went on; and as it did so, its true nature became increasingly evident. The further it advanced, the further back it pushed the traditional orders and institutions, till finally, in our own time, it has achieved its aim and has permeated virtually the whole of life.

A second important turning point in this long course was reached when the new principle spread from the ecclesiastical to the secular sphere, in the form of the organized "state." This took place while the ecclesiastical hierarchy was still in process of development, at the other summit of power in the West, the Empire. The mighty Frederick II, the last of the Hohenstaufen emperors, developed in his Sicilian patrimony the first modern state to be organized according to these principles. Later he extended the new kind of rule over the whole of Italy. The principle of national organization was extended from him, "the first ruler of the modern type who sat upon a throne,"[3] to the Italian states of the Renaissance, and from there to all the states of Europe and, later, of the world. This restructuring of the state according to the principle of organization, which Frederick introduced into Italy, was already strongly marked throughout by the principles of objectivity and of personal individuality, which are always essential to the organization. Till then, a person's distinguishing mark was "only as member of a race, people, party, family, or corporation — only through some general category. In Italy this veil first melted into air; an *objective* treatment and consideration of the state and of all the things of this world became possible. The *subjective* side at the same time asserted itself with corresponding

[3] Jacob Burckhardt, *The Civilization of the Renaissance in Italy,* trans. S. G. C. Middlemore (London: Macmillan Co., 1878), I, 5.

emphasis; man became a spiritual *individual,* and recognized himself as such."[4] That is to say, he recognized himself to be an individual personality. "Observe the expressions 'uomo singolare' and 'uomo unico' for the higher and highest stages of individual development."[5]

The new principle did not come fully into its own, however, until Western man went further, as a logical consequence, along the course that had been plotted and broke open the enveloping womb of ecclesiastical sanctity. The decisive impulse in this direction came from the Reformation. Luther taught that politics, indeed every vocation, "is, so to speak, barred from heaven and applied to earth."[6] In so doing, he cleared the way for another logical development of the organization. It was here in the Reformation that the organization acquired its next permanent basic feature: secularization.

At first the development proceeded mainly within the sphere of the state. The prince, as territorial sovereign, assumed a new status: he was "sovereign" and *legibus absolutus* — that is, he was the untrammeled master of the process of legislation in his country. He recognized, however, that, as he was ruling "by the grace of God," he was responsible before God. In his state, therefore, he occupied the position that the pope had earlier claimed and consolidated in the church; that is, standing as a solitary person before God, he was at once *in* the institution and *above* it. And once again the instrument employed was a hierarchy — the whole apparatus of government authorities and officials, as well as the army. Thus, by hard work and against stiff opposition, the territorial princes extended the principle of organization further and pushed it deeper into the social body of the West than the church had been able to do formerly. At the same time, their subjects' way of life still retained, for the time being, its traditional stratified structure.

Now there came a third advance, and again the principle

[4] *Ibid.,* p. 129.
[5] *Ibid.,* n. 1.
[6] Gustaf Wingren, *Luther on Vocation,* trans. Carl C. Rasmussen (Philadelphia: Muhlenberg Press, 1957), p. 11.

was carried over, lock, stock, and barrel, into a new sphere of human life: work and economics. The figure of the entrepreneur, which had been foreshadowed during the centuries following the Renaissance, has dominated the economic system since the industrial and agricultural reforms of the nineteenth century. It was through the entrepreneur that work moved, on a very wide scale, away from the traditional methods and social orders into the new flexible structures of "the business," and in so doing brought the principle of the organization to fruition here too. Once again it was the individual, acting of set purpose, who broke away from the traditional restrictions of the guilds and other brotherhoods and then, to the extent that he was able, shook off the tutelage of the state, under whose protecting hand he had set out on his course.

This independence of action by the entrepreneurs at first rested largely on a Calvinistic type of Christian faith and Christian self-discipline, as Max Weber has shown in his well-known study, *The Protestant Ethic and the Spirit of Capitalism*.[7] In the early days, when the requisite structure still had to be groped after, it was clearly once again the "person before God" who ventured forth by himself on the new paths. And, once again, a hierarchy was developed, this time within the new structural pattern of "the business." This battery of subordinates was modeled closely after the pattern of the officialdom of the state. With the persons he employed the entrepreneur concluded the "free contract of employment." For most of the employees this meant a formal freedom which put them, in their turn, "on their own." If the industrial and agricultural reforms had set those who were economically independent free from the enveloping grip of the institution and made them individuals in their own right, the "free contract of employment" now did something similar for the broad masses of people who were not economically independent.

In this way the principle of organization, with its inherent

[7] Max Weber, *The Protestant Ethic and the Spirit of Capitalism*, trans. Talcott Parsons (New York: Charles Scribner's Sons, 1930; first published in German in 1904/5).

element of freedom, was carried in a three-pronged advance through the length and breadth of the social structure, if we may leave it at that in this greatly oversimplified picture. More and more people were now freed from the confines of the institution.

Now, however, something else entered the picture, for as the new principle of organization took root, pushing people more and more into the arms of freedom, there also spread through Christendom the claim to individual responsibility. The gospel had indeed addressed its appeal to each one as a person. This had its effect, either open or concealed, in every Christian century, but it blossomed into new and vigorous life in the Reformation. In drawing a distinction between the person and his office, Luther put the individual, in the gospel sense of one responsible before God and his neighbor, *in* that office but also *beside* it and *above* it. Consequently the proto-types who headed the new organizations came to discover that their examples were being widely emulated. Even the popes in the high and late Middle Ages very soon saw their *plenitudo potestatis,* their own exclusive right of decision, contested by the conciliar movement, by heretical movements, and finally by the Reformation. Similarly the territorial sovereigns educated first their officials and then, through them, their "subjects" themselves to critical and independent thought. This in the long run brought with it freedom of expression and the right to share in political life, the end result being that the sovereignty was finally transferred to the populace itself. It is one of the lessons of history that the exclusive right of decision in an organization — in contrast to a sacrosanct, traditional social structure — is not, in the long run, going to remain at the summit.

The great charter and guarantee of this general demand for freedom is today the "rights of man" as the "basic law" of all the liberal constitutions of the world. The idea of these human rights has also grown from Christian roots; it comes from the parliamentary revolution of English puritanism of the seventeenth century. Here the issue was at first not the rights of man as such but "the rights of freedom necessary for the salvation of the elect, who needed them in order to stand fast in their faith while still on earth. It was only later, when they were universalized, that these rights of the saints became the rights of man."[8] Thus we can clearly recognize the Christian origins of freedom: proceeding from the pope, going on to the territorial princes who ruled "by the grace of God" and then to the early entrepreneurs, finally it became the legal right of everyone.

To repeat: in what has been said above, there has been no attempt to trace, even in outline, the tortuous and complicated way in which the "organization" and, at the same time, the freedom of the individual established themselves in European history. Our concern has been simply to expose to view certain outstanding turning points, and to show that in these the Christian faith was a powerful driving force. But we have seen enough to perceive that it is not by chance that Western patterns of life have been reshaped along the same lines as those suggested by the gospel itself. Faith in the gospel was a persistent motive force in these reconstructions — that is, in the creation of the modern organization. Thus the historical development gives us further confirmation of the surprising fact that the present time, together with its social structures, is oriented to the gospel in a special way. That is a fact that cannot and must not be ignored.

The Dismantling of the Old Machinery

The forward march of the "organization" as a new constructive principle had, in some degree, its counterpart or reflection in the dismantling of the sacrosanct, traditional orders and institutions. The processes ran parallel to each other, within the same period of time, and it is essential to our purposes that we again look at them briefly.

While it was being reshaped into an organization by the

---

[8] Hans Dombois, *Naturrecht und christliche Existenz* (Kassel: Johannes Stauda Verlag, 1952), p. 20.

vigorous initiative of the great popes, the Roman Catholic church of the Middle Ages continued to regard itself as a wholly sacrosanct order, an earthly institution for salvation. There was therefore no thought of giving up the appeal to ecclesiastical traditions in doctrine, ministry, and worship; on the contrary, the development went ahead cautiously on the basis of existing traditions, with the object of allowing any innovations to become traditions themselves. It is to this discreet mixture of tradition and innovation that the Roman Catholic church owes its present admirable stability. At first, therefore, the impetus towards secularization was not evident in the organization called "church," and the impetus towards flexibility was only very limited.

In contrast to this, the state was already exhibiting more clearly the specific qualities of an organization. In early modern times the world of the state was the scene of change and movement. New aims were consciously pursued, and their achievement often involved extreme ruthlessness towards the old ones. We need only think of the creation of the autocracy in France under Louis XIV and Richelieu, where the standing army and the mercantile system were developed in the pursuit of power politics. Other examples are the building up of Russia under the three great Hohenzollerns, and the far-reaching transformation of Russia under the restless and masterful hand of Peter the Great. Here the principle of the organization developed its dynamic nature in an impressive way.

Secularization, too, progressed inexorably in the state. For if all the rules and regulations became so flexible and so subservient to the ends in view, they could no longer possess any innate sanctity. The administrative apparatus of the state assumed those prosaic characteristics with which we are familiar today.

At the head of the State, as regards the persons and symbols that represented the state as a whole, it was a different matter. Here there was invariably the "hallowed person of the monarch," the sanctity of the throne, the religious oath binding one to service of the state. Corresponding to all this was the intimate union of the state and the territorial church, and, in the German Protestant churches, the establishment of the supreme episcopacy with the territorial prince as the archbishop of his territorial church. It was the oft-cited alliance of "throne and altar" that was expressed in such formulas as "For God, king, and country," or in the patriotic religious songs and calls to arms, for instance, in the German wars of liberation of 1813–14. The crown, and therefore the fatherland, was surrounded by a religious halo; here a sacrosanct institution lived on for a long time.

Now, however, there emerged something that no organization — according to all the lessons of history — can escape in the long run: a limitation of its powers. The great reform popes, of all people, had still claimed an unfettered power over men, though in fact they had not been able to enforce the claim. The state now began to experience limitations placed on its powers, the restrictions becoming more marked as time went on. It was the Enlightenment of the seventeenth and eighteenth centuries, advocating reasoned and critical thought in all areas of life, which demanded that the state should reserve to its citizens their own private and inviolable sphere of judgment, and then should respect that sphere. Here, too, originated the idea of the division of powers (Locke, Montesquieu), which split up the state structure, hitherto thought to be indivisible, into several parts, each with its own limited sphere of action. This idea of a balance of powers among the legislature, the judiciary, and the executive has since become a principle underlying all the liberal constitutions of the world. The libertarian movement was a factor that served to limit the state's powers still further. In the early years of libertarianism young Wilhelm von Humboldt (1767–1835) wrote an essay that in its very title spoke of "an attempt to determine the limits of the state's functions."

The guaranteeing of a private sphere, the division of powers, and the narrowing of the state's powers all had the same object; and here, in the development of the state, appeared in the plainest and most effective way the last and most important feature of the "organization": the liberation of the person. The clearest expression of this is the legal history of the modern state in the eighteenth and nineteenth centuries. This significant process can be seen in the great legal codifications of this period, especially the "General Common Law for the Prussian States" of 1794 and the Austrian "General Civil Legal Code" of 1811. These codifications are much more than interesting episodes in legal history. In fact, the lengthy development we have described earlier in this chapter was here carried to its weighty logical conclusion in the legal, and therefore in the institutional, social, and political spheres. Till then, man in his relation to the law, and therefore to the institution, had been governed by the institution. His station in life determined what he was. On a broad view, "in the Middle Ages one's legal standing was made to depend on his station in the community, which rested on family, occupation, and descent. The fact of belonging to a particular group determined the individual's legal status and therefore his legal capacity."[9] That means that, under the social system of the time, a man was not regarded, and did not regard himself, as an "individual." "The main thing was the association to which the individual belonged . . . . The law had no occasion to bring individual existence into a special category of rights and duties."[10] An individual's legal right, and therefore his ability, to maintain institutional relationships with others was rooted in the institution itself, and not in his having any free and independent status in relation to it. Social reality resided in the institution, not in the person. Things were still just as Wilhelm Grönbech described them when he wrote of the German tribal ties, and the same state of affairs existed in all institutions everywhere, before the worldwide revolutionary breakthrough of the legal development in Western countries, which has brought universal freedom in relation to the institu-

[9] Hermann Conrad, *Individuum und Gemeinschaft in der Privatrechtsordnung des 18. und beginnenden 19. Jahrhunderts* ("Schriftenreihe der Juristischen Studiengesellschaft Karlsruhe," No. 18 [Karlsruhe, 1956]), p. 6.
[10] Eugen Huber, cited in *ibid.*, p. 6.

tion. Now "the individual was freed from the legal fetters of socially stratified communities . . . and from the legal bonds imposed by religion, and was made a legal entity in relation to the state."[11] Hegel could now set out, as one of the law's main axioms, "Be a person, and respect others as persons." Indeed, the law actually became a "weapon of the individual."[12]

Thus the position that had formerly been taken by the popes and the sovereign territorial princes — within the institution and yet standing over against it — was now transferred by law to all men, at any rate wherever these legal systems held jurisdiction. A legal basis had been created on which it was no longer possible for any comprehensive sacrosanct orders and institutions to exist; room was left only for organizations. We have here the same thing as appeared in "human rights," namely, universal "individual existence" (Eugen Huber). Although, as we saw, the Christian faith was discernible as the ultimate root of the matter, it must now be added that the place where the new structure of existence was most fully realized was the state, and that the historical movement through which the idea finally triumphed was the Enlightenment of the eighteenth century.

Thus it was the maturing state, together with its legal development, which in the course of centuries cleared away the whole remaining structure of traditional, ecclesiastically buttressed orders and institutions. The rise of the modern state after the Renaissance and the Reformation was characterized by a conscious striving to unite at a single point all the power contained within a particular geographical area. The territorial prince alone was to have power of determination, and the authority to use his powers at his own discretion. All social entities within the territory were to understand that they lived only at his good pleasure. He set out to be the sole social and political reality; no municipality, no village brotherhood, no manorial court, and no provincial diet was now to live and

[11] Conrad, *op. cit.*, p. 7.
[12] See Heinrich Mitteis, "Das Recht als Waffe des Individuums," *Die Rechtsidee in der Geschichte* (Weimar, 1957), pp. 514 ff.

make decisions according to the law of its particular rank and class. It was the very same claim that the pope had formerly made within the church, with which he had turned it into a hierarchy of officials. In the same way the territorial prince now tried to bring the stratified society of his day into his service, and to shape it into his instrument.

The absolutist state of the seventeenth and eighteenth centuries was only partly successful in this attempt. Within that stratified society there were minorities that insisted defiantly on their traditional rights. But they manned isolated posts, with no prospects of victory. From the French Revolution onward, the lines of development had led in the direction of the constitutional state, and the time was ripe for abandoning the antiquated and moribund remains of the institutions of that society of ranks and classes. In the early decades of the nineteenth century, at the same time that the "Holy Roman Empire of the German Nation" was collapsing under Napoleon's blows, the state reforms were carried through which put an end to the old empire's traditional stratified society. The so-called emancipation of the serfs meant the dissolution of the old ties of village brotherhoods, which had kept agricultural production in bondage to traditional methods of work and had allowed no initiative for introducing modern means of production. The same period saw the end of the feudal ties, which had once been a sound political arrangement but which were meaningless and cramping in a modern state. Similarly, in the towns handicraft and trade were released from the institutional ties of guilds and corporations, again so as to give free play to initiative.

Thus the ground was prepared, the field was cleared, and the structural patterns were prefigured. A new social world was not only possible — it was inevitable.

The Coming of a New World

This new social world is our world. It is our lot to work in it, and we do our best to understand it. It is often called the "industrial society," because we see it dominated by the new labor and production techniques of industry, whereas the old stratified society was organized for peasants, landed estates, and handicrafts. Accordingly, the whole development of the new world has been called a process of "industrialization," and the same process in Asia, Africa, and Latin America is still so described. Indeed, the beginning of industrialization has been given the name "Industrial Revolution," and it is supposed, in conjunction with political revolution, and especially the French Revolution of 1789, to have changed the world.

We have already suggested that the nineteenth-century upheaval was of such profound significance as to be comparable only to an immense change in the distant past: the transition from a nomadic and hunting existence to agrarian settlements about five thousand years ago. Just as there was a transition then from "prey" to "harvest," so now there is one to "production."[13] Now, as then, man's whole relationship to himself, to nature, to other men, and to the unseen powers, has been revolutionized.

What has so far been discussed has already provided us with a few standards with which to verify these statements. Accordingly, we find that if we try to define the great upheaval in terms of "industry," the definition is superficial and inadequate. For it denotes at best an important external aspect of a phenomenon, but it does not really go to the heart of the matter. Everything suggests that it would be more accurate to speak of a "personal revolution" and a "personal society"; these terms might well express much more adequately the nature and significance of the upheaval. But to substantiate this thesis we need to look still further into the course of the upheaval and the direction in which it developed. Our world is still caught up in this process, or at least in its consequences, and it is not till our twentieth century that we can distinguish more clearly the phenomena that can justify the use of the term "personal society."

As regards the profound nature of the upheaval, too, any

[13] Hans Schomerus, *Realistisches Leben* (Stuttgart, 1958).

comparison with the establishment of man's first settlements, that profound change in the distant past, must be open to question. There are many points of resemblance, and the indication that the comparison gives of the extraordinary importance of the upheaval is valuable; it keeps one from misunderstanding or minimizing what the nineteenth century brought into the world. If we have to go so far back for a comparison, we see the immensity of the whole affair. Yet the comparison must seem strange when we remember that the nineteenth-century upheaval had a remote source, and that it was a result and consequence of the gospel. In the concise words of the legal historian Heinrich Mitteis, "Man's confinement to a group was finally abolished only by the influence of Christianity."[14] If we feel it impossible to imagine this radical desacralizing of the world and this liberation of the individual without the immensely tough and powerful two-thousand-year-old gospel, then we can see the nineteenth century as merely one phase in a single, unique, and incomparable development in the history of mankind. In that case the comparison with the establishment of the first settlements, instead of emphasizing the immense significance of this development, must unduly minimize it.

Within this whole development the nineteenth-century phase was distinctive, to be sure. What had been in the making during long centuries of preparation now erupted with primitive force. What had long been germinating almost or entirely unseen broke on the world with a sudden and unprecedented outburst of fecundity. One may venture to assert that in respect to fruitfulness in the creation of new social structures, no other period of world history is even remotely comparable to the nineteenth century. But everything had a common denominator: the principle of organization took sudden and firm hold of the entire life of the people, and in doing so assumed the most varied shapes; it produced entirely new social structures, or transformed existing ones both at their core and in their outward appearance.

[14] Mitteis, *op. cit.*, p. 519.

The nineteenth century is generally known as a time of numerous and revolutionary technical inventions. What is easily overlooked is that it was also the century of numerous and revolutionary social inventions. What a wealth of organizations there were, at the end of the century, which at its beginning were either totally unknown or only in embryo: the most varied kinds of industrial enterprises, joint stock companies, private insurance companies and social insurance provided by the state, political parties, trade unions, agricultural and industrial cooperatives on lines suggested by Friedrich-Wilhelm Raiffeisen and Franz-Hermann Schulze-Delitzsch, consumers' cooperatives modeled on that of the Rochdale weavers of England, hobby clubs, special-interest groups, complex educational systems (based in part on the reforms of Wilhelm von Humboldt), technical colleges, new kinds of military organizations such as the general staff created by Gerhard von Scharnhorst, self-governing corporations following the ideas of Franz von Stein in towns and rural districts, professional societies, craft guilds, railroad companies, states with constitutional monarchy or parliamentary monarchy or universal suffrage, church institutions for social work such as the Bethel colonies of Friedrich von Bodelschwingh. The list could be extended indefinitely and in detail, but it will serve to show the nineteenth century's unprecedented productivity with respect to social structures. It is clear, too, from the names that we have mentioned, that here in the social sphere we also have inventions and inventors, even as in the development of machines, steel production, production and transmission of electricity, and agricultural methods.

Looking back, we can now clearly distinguish two phases in the creation and development of this new social world; observing this distinction will help us considerably in keeping our bearings. The first phase was the stormy period of initial construction, the quick succession of new inventions and the appearance of new phenomena. It was the time of conflict between the old system, which had not yet expired, and the new. The separate new phenomena stood uncoordinated alongside one another, and the consequence was severe tensions and deep chasms: entrepreneur and laborer, agriculture and industry, town and village, handicraft and industry, entrepreneur and state were often at odds with each other, and government regulation could do little more than laboriously paper over the cracks. Moreover, the new structures themselves were still untested, and were handled without any deftness of touch. There were as yet no new models for the way life was to be lived in a changing world. The old models persisted — the benevolent patriarchal master, the devoted servant, the housewife confined to her house — but they receded further and further as they corresponded less and less to changing realities. On the other side there was unfolded a kaleidoscopic assortment of "movements" thrusting their way out of old or new shackles, for example, the cooperative movement, the labor movement, the women's emancipation movement, the youth movement, the nationalistic movements within the old imperial structures of Austria, Russia, and Turkey. But lesser aims were also pursued that took on the form of "movements": the movement for small, family gardens, the movement for better living conditions, and so on.

Then occurred, in the first half of the twentieth century, what discerning critics had long feared: an epoch of "movements" and of fragmented and uncoordinated development ended in a period of frightful catastrophes. The storm clouds of the political and social revolution in Russia in 1905 were the prelude, followed by the First World War, revolutions, national upheavals, the collapse of old empires, inflation, the world economic crisis, and finally the Second World War with its criminal and devastating consequences and accompanying phenomena — mass murders and bombings, concentration and internment camps, mass displacements of peoples and floods of refugees.

We do not yet know whether this series of great and devastating catastrophes will go on, or even get worse, or whether we may be granted a period of comparative stability. This much, however, can be said: the old industrial nations have, paradoxically, taken their place as part of the modern world precisely during the recent catastrophic decades; they have built up and coordinated their world of modern technology and organization to the point that they feel at home in it. The circle of possible and necessary types of organizations seems to have been closed without any great gaps. As we shall see later, the changes needed concern mainly the extension and improvement of existing types, and are rarely anything new. Cracks and tensions still exist, but if we look at people's ordinary lives, we get a different picture from that prior to 1914. To give just a few more examples: When the stock phrases of class war crop up now, they are felt to be out-of-date. The gap between rich and poor has been narrowed by an extensive leveling of incomes, and blurred by ease of passage from one class to the next. Despite all forebodings, craftsmanship has again created an assured status for itself alongside industry. Rural areas are becoming urbanized, and city people are increasingly moving out from the core of the city to more sparsely settled areas. In brief, as far as the older industrial nations are concerned, the conditions for stabilizing the new social world seem to exist. It could be that the period of stormy and disjointed development will be followed by one of consolidation and integration.

To be sure, this division of periods holds good only for the old industrial nations. Alongside these, in the communist world and among the nonwhite peoples, a process of "industrialization," that is, of "organization," is taking place. And although in many respects this process has assumed a modified form and is driven by other forces, it is clear that that world too is going through a period of agitated and impassioned development like the one that the old industrial nations have just been through. Unrest has therefore not left the world, but only shifted its center to other parts of the world.

The Basic Types of the New Order

The individualizing of man, which initially consisted merely in his faith as an "individual soul before God," was first brought over into the institutional world by the state. It re-

65

garded, and addressed, its "subjects" (later its "citizens") as a sum of individuals, and it still does so. Legal development had been in accordance with this, granting every individual the same standing, namely, as a "person," that is, one who has rights.[15] Closely related to this development were the governmental reforms that had abolished the old brotherhoods and feudal ties in town and country. One might think that with all this the old structures were completely done away with. But that was not so. The real nucleus of that old world, its basic unit, continued to exist; the "household" was still the smallest social unit of human life.

The old world with its stratified society had been essentially an institutional world. Life in that world was constituted and governed by institutional regulations, not by individual responsibility. For that reason, the cornerstone was bound to be not the individual, but an institution; and that institution was the "household," or, as people then said, "the whole household." It was of "whole households," not of individuals, that the peasants' communities of the mark system, the towns and guilds, the manors and feudal estates were composed. The state itself at one time emerged from the "house" of the territorial sovereign.

It was not only the stratified society of the medieval world that had been built up in this way on the basis of the household. The ancient and biblical worlds, too, had had their nucleus, their smallest building stone, in the *oikos,* that domestic community which was often very comprehensive, and which included the slaves as well.

The most important characteristics of the "whole household" for our present purposes were, first, that it was a community of life in all its aspects, with a virtually unlimited number of duties, and, secondly, that in relation to the outside world the members of the house did not represent themselves in legal, political, ecclesiastical, economic, and other matters, but were under the care and protection of the master of the house, and were represented by him in dealings with outsiders.

[15] Conrad, *op. cit.*

In medieval Europe the prototype of the "whole household" was the farm household, which over the centuries served as a model for the households of craftsmen and tradesmen, and also, with appropriate modifications, for the aristocratic houses of the nobility. Common to all, however, was the indissoluble unity of family life and vocational life. To these were added as a matter of course such further concerns as education, care of the old and sick, and social life. The household was the place where people lived and died, where they spent their time together during and after the day's work, where the children worked and played together and grew up to take their place in the adult world, which they would take over as loyally and with as little change as possible, to hand it on, when the time came, to their own children. It will be seen, then, that the household was generally a large one. Besides the parents and children, also living there would be the grandparents, unmarried uncles and aunts, journeymen and apprentices, manservants and maidservants. The large number of duties meant a correspondingly large number of people.

As long as people earned their living as farmers and craftsmen, the "whole household" remained the real pattern of life in the small circle. And as long as that was true, the new legal system with its "individual person" did not yet correspond to the realities of social life. The two did not really begin to dovetail until vocational life moved out of the household and was concentrated and remodeled in the shape of "business." For now the man at work was severed every day from the "household" for as long as he was working; a "free contract of employment" was made with him as an individual; and with these individuals as the stones of the building, the business could now be an "organization," that is, it could be built up, enlarged, reduced, or restructured to achieve the desired goals. Places of employment at a distance from home had always existed; in earlier centuries, for instance, mines and factories had assembled considerable numbers of workers at a place that was not their home. But that had been exceptional. Even into the nineteenth century, as during thousands of years before it, work was done primarily within the household, which was thus the actual basic unit of the social system, however diverse the structure of the latter in other respects.

But now the removal of work outside the confines of the household meant that the nucleus of the old order of society was also split, and this "splitting of the atom" — the metaphor taken from nuclear physics is quite appropriate here — set in motion a chain reaction of cause and effect that ended by completely changing the substance, that is, the constitution, of society. For the world of "businesses" now expanded with great rapidity and in an uncommon diversity of ways. This was intensified with the coming of the use of machines, which, in conjunction with the division of labor, required entirely new methods of work, these in their turn necessitating entirely new forms of organization.

In another way, too, the separation of work from the household was not without consequences. Such a loss meant that the household was no longer a "whole household"; indeed, it soon became obviously no "household" at all, for it took on an entirely different pattern. The separation of work and household had considerably reduced the domestic community, and for this and other reasons the household proceeded to transfer many other tasks to other, new social bodies. What finally remained was a social structure of a new kind, the "family," which generally consisted only of parents and un-married children, and which lived in a "dwelling," whether in an apartment house or in a house of its own. That is the family as we now know it, and we could easily suppose that that particular structure had existed from time immemorial as inherent in the human situation. But that is true only in a very limited sense. Of course, the relationship of father, mother, and child is one of the fundamental realities of human existence, as it is predetermined by our physical nature. But as a matter of history, this basic relationship has been expressed in quite different ways in different periods of human history. One of these ways was the "household" in the specific form that it assumed in the Christian Middle Ages. Another is the present-day small family, which is by no means without its problems, and whose development does not yet appear to be complete.

Alongside family and business, there appeared in the nineteenth century a third basic structural type that was embodied in a great variety of forms: the "association" [*Verein*]. Whereas hitherto there had been but little banding together of this nature (scientific societies, brotherhoods of journeymen, fraternities of students from the same geographical area at the universities), the association suddenly blossomed out into a very effective kind of organization. At first the state had prohibited the extension of this social structure, for the principle of the absolutist state stood in contradiction to any voluntary banding together for self-chosen ends decided on by a majority of the members. But the nineteenth-century state accommodated itself with more or less reluctance even to the liberal forms of parliamentary government, and it had to give way also to its citizens' insistent pressure for the right to band together in "associations."

But hardly had the right of association, and with it the necessary right of assembly, been wrung from the state when in a very short space of time thousands upon thousands of associations sprang up out of the ground, and the citizens' long-stifled personal initiative found here ample opportunities for pursuing the most varied kinds of aims. This unlimited variety and comprehensive significance of the organizational principle of "association" are still with us. That is at once evident when one stops to think what diverse activities, under what different names, are rooted in this basic type. The whole world of the great associations representing the interests of employers and employees in the economic sphere belong here, as do the political parties, the cooperatives of all kinds, youth groups, athletic clubs, church societies, women's clubs, campus fraternities, and anything else that is called a society, union, club, study group, circle, league, alliance, convention, and so on. In spite of the official obligation to register with the government, at least for those associations that desire to be "persons in the eyes of the law," this whole kaleidoscopic world of organiza-

69

tions eludes all systematic ordering and enumeration. In the association the wealth and variety of concerns, aims, aspirations, and interests that are part of modern life can be pursued through a medium of common action that is flexible and infinitely variable. For all these different creations, so varied in size, aspiration, and composition, are in the final analysis based on the same simple design: the voluntary association of individuals who join together to achieve certain specified aims, and who choose their own instruments for carrying these out, the structure and the rules of the association being open to change at any time on a majority decision.

We are dealing, then, once again with an "organization" pure and simple. Indeed, when people talk of an organization, they are often thinking primarily of an association or a federation and imagine that these terms are completely synonymous. But that is not the case. For a business is also an organization; but a business and an association exhibit the same principle of organization in exactly opposite ways. The business in all its varied forms, whether a repair shop, a bank, a railroad company, or a coal mine, rests on decisions that are made at the top and transmitted downward; the direction of affairs is with the management. In an association, on the other hand, the leadership takes its orders from the members as a whole, the final authority being the general meeting of members. Attempts to build up a business on the structural principle of the association, to establish so-called producers' cooperatives, have often been made, but with few exceptions they have failed. For this kind of work, the most suitable organizational structure seems to be direction from above, whereas representation of the common interest seems to require direction from below.

In the Middle Ages authority and brotherhood were, as they have always been, two basic patterns of the shaping of human institutions, from the monarchies and republics of the ancient world to the Germanic peoples' assembly called the *Thing* and the tyranny of the mounted Mongolians. Both of these basic patterns have reappeared — in the form of the "business" and the "association" — in the new structural principle of the "organization," and they still dominate our lives today. Certainly, there are important changes going on, bringing the two types ever closer together with the passage of time. We shall return to these changes later.

"Family," "business," and "association" do not exhaust the list of basic types in modern society, for besides these we have to include the state with its institutions. The state had been the first to develop the principle of organization in the secular sphere; and it was on that model, especially in respect to its officialdom organized in administrative units, that the large businesses and corporations created their own administrative machinery. But while that was happening, the state itself changed its face. In place of monarchical rule, there emerged on all sides the principle of the sovereignty of the people, and with it the principle of making decisions and issuing instructions from the bottom upward. It was expressed everywhere in a central legislative body, and, in many states, in the machinery of self-government. But now the development of our new highly diversified modern society, in the basic structures of the business and the association, has presented the state with a great and growing number of new problems. An industrialized, mechanized society poses problems different from those of a society of peasants and craftsmen, with its economy centered in the household and governed by the traditions and customs of rank and class — the society in which the subjects of the absolutist state lived, even in the eighteenth century.

To tackle the multiplicity of new problems with which it was now faced, the state had to develop and greatly extend its official machinery, and add departments of quite a new kind. Again to mention only a few examples: departments dealing with architecture, labor, commerce and transportation, finance (an area greatly extended by the state's increasing responsibilities), the administration of justice (entailing new duties in connection with industrial, administrative, and financial tribunals), health and welfare, culture (involving museums and other institutions), education and its varied and specialized school systems, and so on. We can see that the state has played a very significant role in the immense task of creating new institutions in the nineteenth and twentieth centuries.

In the state, and in its various departments, the same two principles established themselves that were first seen clearly as fundamentally distinct in the business and the association: the directive from above and authorization from below. Thus for a long time there was in the state a strange conjunction of sacrosanct aura and sober organization. As we have said, the state had drawn to itself and assimilated the sacrosanct self-sufficiency of all other institutions; and so it was that it kept longer than any other institution its sacrosanct, or rather pseudosacrosanct, aura. To this day the state has remained an ambiguous entity; for although it has long been the doughtiest champion of the new principle of organization, it has kept longest with its secular regulations the typical features of a sacrosanct institution, though indeed these have been steadily on the decline.

The same thing holds good for the family, which, of course, is not really to be regarded as an "organization." One enters a business or an association by means of a simple contract, or by a straightforward declaration. For the civil service an oath is still required. The family, too, generally still begins at the altar; it also usually goes to church to celebrate the most important stages in its existence. At the same time both state and family exhibit the characteristics of the organization: limited authority, flexibility in structure, and the freeing of the individual member through the fact that some essential parts of his life do not belong to it.

All in all, then, we can distinguish four basic types into which the varied structures of modern life can be fitted: the family, the business, the association, and the state with its various departments. These four types cannot be traced back to one another; they have grown up out of permanent factors of human existence as if out of conditions laid down by history. But they do enable us to reduce the bewildering variety of our social system to a few large groups. The most important thing, however, is not the classification itself, but its enabling us to see and understand clearly the development that is presently under way. For changes certainly are from time to time taking place within, and in relation to, the basic types. Individual changes that are widely diffused and difficult to survey can thus be brought together in one place and understood as variations of one main theme. In the chapters which follow, therefore, we shall draw in rough outline a picture (which is never static) of the association, the business, and the state, one after another, as they are today. The family we shall deal with in detail in a later chapter.

To conclude, we may remark that of course the types are not always clear-cut, that there is often blending and overlapping. Thus an insurance company may be established as a "society based on mutual agreement," yet display all the characteristics of a business in its office organization with a manager and staff. A transport undertaking such as a state railway is just as much a business as a government department of public law, in which a great many of the employees have the status of officials. A farm where the work is still done by the family is at once a family and a business in the modern sense of the words; it cannot now be simply a "household" in the old sense.

We cannot, then, pin down every entity as belonging simply to one single type. In fact, we shall see that the differences are in process of shading off into each other to a quite remarkable extent, even as between the basic types. In all of them are simultaneously developing certain features which identify them as belonging to the same historical epoch, and which also justify the use of the homogeneous term "organization."

Questions To Be Raised

In order that the forest may not be obscured by the trees, we must ask plainly what our investigation of the present basic types of organization is intended to make clear. There are two sets of questions that emerge from what we have said so far.

1) The old sacrosanct and traditional orders and institutions in the Middle Ages and early modern times gave human corporate life great stability. When the world went over to the new secularized flexible order based on the principle of organization, it meant the decline of the old system with its cohesive and regulative structural patterns. Has this delivered the world up to a do-as-you-please instability? Or are there now appearing cohesive forces that provide — or, shall we say, that can provide — this new and very mobile world with stability of a new kind? If so, what sort of forces are these?

2) In the historical development as we have surveyed it, the "individualizing" process stands out clearly as the obverse of the downgrading of the old sacrosanct institutions. What has not been clearly delineated thus far is the nature of the process, though the fact of its taking place is incontrovertible. It is to be hoped, however, that what is involved in this individualizing may be discerned from the picture of the present structure. The second group of questions, therefore, considers these problems: In what way is modern man an "individual" in the social world? How, and how far, is the social pattern designed to require, or perhaps allow, him to act as an individual? What is his own attitude towards this? Does he feel the individualizing to be a burden or a right?

It will be seen that the answers to these two groups of questions converge to give us a statement of our own position. Before the actual discussion begins, however, we have to touch on a related topic that is playing a decisive part in the development as a whole: the population question.

4

Population Fluctuation as

Cause and Key

Population growth is of special interest to us primarily in two respects: first as a powerful motive force, in fact, as a relentless pressure to change to new structures of life; and then as a consequence and expression of the transition from an institutional to a personal society. Here is what we mean.

The population of a country may be thought of not simply as a fixed sum of individuals, not even as a changing sum, but as a process, an ongoing dynamic process involving births and deaths, immigration and emigration. Now, in the human sphere no phenomena are solely natural — they all bear the stamp of history as well as of nature. It is obvious to everyone that immigration and emigration are determined historically. So too the natural increase resulting from an excess of births over deaths, while it is a natural phenomenon, is by no means determined entirely by the natural factors of physical life. In any given period it too is shaped by specific historical conditions. Thus population growth has in a special way both accompanied and undergirded the great upheaval of the nineteenth and twentieth centuries, thus reflecting clearly the various phases of the development discussed in the preceding chapters.

The Pressure of Increasing Population

If we look merely at the matter of size, we find that on the whole population changed slowly and over long periods during the era that was dominated by institutions and social stratification. It was only some special catastrophes, such as the Black Death or the Thirty Years' War, that decimated the population quickly; but in a few decades it was back to what it had been before. On the other hand, population increased whenever new space for living and for food production was opened up: by the emergence of towns in the high Middle Ages; by colonization eastward; by the diking of fenlands; by settlement and cultivation of mountainous areas. As we said, these were slow movements over long periods; but they revealed a striking fact: population tended to adjust itself to the available *"Lebensraum"* ("living space"). *Lebensraum* does not refer merely to geographical space; it refers also to the way in which that space is used, and to the prevailing structure of social and economic life.

At about the end of the eighteenth century and the beginning of the nineteenth, the rural population began to increase very rapidly; this quickly led to overcrowding in the villages, and to grinding poverty on a wide scale. The distress was perceived and, in the parlance of the time, was designated "pauperism." The old economic and social structures were no longer adequate to support the explosive growth in the number of human beings. The *Lebensraum* grew too confined. There were only two ways out, and both were taken, one after the other. The first was emigration. From 1820 to 1914, for example, five and a half million Germans left their homeland. The second was a transition to the new economic and social structures of "industrial" society. This way, taken increasingly in Germany from the middle of the century on, made it possible not only to support, within the very same area, a population that increased almost threefold between 1816 and 1910, but even to provide it with a higher standard of living. (In the territory of the German Reich there were 23.5 million people in 1871, and 64.9 million in 1910.) In all the old industrial countries this pressure of a rapidly growing population hastened and, indeed, compelled the great upheaval of the nineteenth and twentieth centuries. Today the populations of these countries are again at a fairly steady level, or else show a moderate natural increase. The three phases — a slow adjustment over a long period, a rapid increase, and then a return to equilibrium — correspond to the general life cycle of any dynamic process.

Behind the forcible and rapid industrialization of the Soviet Union there was the same compelling need to support an immense surplus rural population; the same is true today in China, India, and many other countries that find themselves in social upheaval as they change from a society based on peasantry and crafts to one based on bureaucracy and industry. At the time of the First World War the empire of the czars had an excess of rural population, which no reform had been able to deal with adequately. For a long time China's population has been increasing by leaps and bounds; whereas the figure is estimated to have been about 330 million in 1872, it must by now exceed 600 million. The case is similar in India, where there are now nearly 500 million mouths to be fed, instead of the (estimated) 175 million in 1855. In such a situation there are again only the two possibilities of avoiding widespread distress: either emigration (which today, however, offers only limited scope even for Europeans, and hardly any for the nonwhite peoples), or great social upheaval.

The Change in the "Generative Structure"

Population growth is of importance for us here not only as a motive force and an accompanying phenomenon of the great social upheaval. It also illustrates in lucid fashion the very process that is the theme of the whole of this book: the dissolution of institutional constraint, and the liberation for responsible personal decisions. For if the level of the population now has something of the stability that it had before the upheaval, it is for quite different reasons. In the stratified society of the past the picture of the "generative structure" or "population pattern," namely, the combined effect of the three factors, marriage, birth, and death, was quite different from what it is today. In Germany, for instance — in other countries it was much the same, although with characteristic modifications — one could marry only if one had a "place" [*Stelle*] of one's own, that is, a farm, a handicraft household, or something of the kind. Anyone who had no "place," either by inheritance or by marriage, had to conform to the law of the social order of the time, which forbade him to marry and to have children. It is characteristic of the institutional and nonpersonal nature of those times that the people who were excluded from marriage actually did conform; they regarded it as self-evident that the order was a reality that determined their manner of life. Besides, there were other established institutions ready to receive them: the farm where they had grown up, or the monastery, or the bands of mercenaries or standing armies. Moreover, an established moral order supported by the church saw to it that the number of illegitimate children remained small.

The number of legitimate children could not be planned and was not planned; it was generally high, though a great many of those who were born were carried off by illness before they were old enough to work or to marry. That, again, limited the number of actual descendants.

The number of "places," however, was determined by the *Lebensraum,* that is, by the available geographical space and the prevailing economic and social order. If the *Lebensraum* expanded through colonization or through the emergence of new means of livelihood, the number of "places" would increase; if it contracted, there would be fewer farms, handicraft establishments, and the like. Thus the natural fertility that is always ready to break all bounds, even among human beings, was held firmly in check. The three factors — marriage, birth, and death — in a way balanced each other, and kept the

78

country's population in a tolerable relation to the available *Lebensraum*. Birth and death remained relatively constant, as at that time there was not much that could be done to control them. The adjustment of population to *Lebensraum* was brought about by way of the one factor that could be controlled: the frequency of marriage. And the frequency of marriage was determined by an institutional system.

The great increase in population began when the children of the "little people" in the country broke away from the rule about having a "place." Young people who, according to the hitherto accepted order, would have had to remain unmarried, scraped together a modest living and started a family. They were able to do this through the spread of the system whereby work was contracted to be done in the home, and through the introduction of the potato, which greatly increased the yield of the arable land. All this provided only a very scanty existence, but people could just make out on it and bring up children.

At first, then, it was only a matter of claiming, as before, a more extensive *Lebensraum*. The new factor, however, was that the old order of society had grown old and stiff, and could not meet the new conditions (or some of the older conditions either, for that matter). What happened, therefore, was not that new "places" were created and fitted into the existing system, but rather that young people defiantly broke away from the existing social order, which was now felt to be "wrong." A claim to equal rights, and to the right of personal decision, was raised, and this, as it developed on a large scale, breached the old order at a vital point. The number of marriages increased, and with it the number of children. The movement spread when the principle of the "place" collapsed with the emancipation of the serfs and the freedom to determine one's own occupation; marriage became open to everyone. Then when industry in its new shape offered great numbers of new jobs, the surplus masses left the country for the towns with their new possibilities of life and marriage, and so the number of births rose still further.

One result of the disintegration of the old social and economic structures and of the freeing of the individual to make decisions apart from the dictates of the institution has been an immense, undreamt-of release of the power to propagate, which had previously been held down by institutional strictures. But this power to propagate is not freed from all barriers. We have already seen that the period of the immense leap in population in the industrial countries has been followed by a new stability in the population level, with the total population remaining steady or increasing only moderately. This new stability stems from a new "generative structure": that is, the three factors of marriage, birth, and death have interacted to produce a new and harmonious "population pattern." They do not rush along blindly and independently of each other — they interact, and together form a living structure.

The stabilizing factor now is not the institution, as it was in the old stratified society, but the decision of the individual. In other words, precisely that force which was so strong and intractable as to break open the old order at a vital spot now shows itself capable of playing a new part, namely, that of a regulator that sets up standards and establishes limits. What are these?

In the new interplay of marriage, birth, and death, the first and the third developed into fairly constant factors. Marriage became general. Today in the Federal Republic of Germany, for example, no more than about ten percent of persons aged forty or above are still single; one can marry if he has almost any kind of work. The average age of death is also tending to reach a natural limit. About 1875 only about one in four of those born in the German Reich lived to be sixty-five, whereas the corresponding figure now in the Federal Republic is two out of three. However, life expectancy cannot be extended indefinitely by hygiene and medicine. We are therefore left with one variable factor: fertility. This, however, has completely changed its character. As we need no longer expect a great many children to die young, the "existence value" of the individual birth[1] has greatly increased; and parents have responded by deliberately restricting the number of births. That is the background of the "decline of the birth rate," which has sometimes given rise to cries of alarm, although it is actually just a logical consequence of the increased expectation of life. Since about 1900 the birth rate in Germany has been steadily declining from about thirty-five to thirty-eight births per thousand inhabitants annually to its present fairly stable level of about sixteen per thousand. Between these figures there are some significant fluctuations: the birth rate fell during the years of the economic crisis that was preceded by the boom of the twenties and followed by that of the thirties.

In the reduction, as well as in the fluctuations corresponding to the economic and political situation (the *"Lebensraum"*), we can see the impact of the new phenomenon of "planned parenthood." Today it is the relation of the number of inhabitants to the *Lebensraum,* and not the number of available "places" (that is, the number of marriages), that determines the deliberately planned number of legitimate births. But planned parenthood is a matter of personal decision, and not of institutional control. And the course of events has shown that such personal decision (which cannot be directed from outside to any appreciable extent), expressed in the population at large, can produce a sound and stable equilibrium between the factors that affect population. Here personal decision is constantly operative at a vital point in our society. With respect to an important sphere of life, then, we have one of our first answers to the question about the stabilizing forces in our mobile society.

Against this background, we can now work out the structural features and developments of modern society by reference to its basic structures. In doing this, it will serve our purposes to take as the first type the association [*Verein*], because there the essential points can be seen most plainly.

[1] Günther Ipsen, "Bevölkerungslehre," *Handwörterbuch des Grenz- und Auslanddeutschtums,* I (Breslau: Ferdinand Hirt, 1933), 425 ff.

5

Associations and

Federations

The far-reaching significance in our society of the basic type designated in chapter three as "association," and the great variety of forms it encompasses, have already been mentioned. This significance simply cannot be overestimated.

It would be well to begin our discussion by delineating the main structural features of the "association," which is the integrating type underlying the many variations on the basic pattern. In the Federal Republic of Germany certain paragraphs (21–79) in the Civil Code lay down the legal form of the association and are binding on all registered associations. This common basis in law justifies our sociological method of tracing such diverse entities back to one single basic type.[1]

What, then, does an association look like from the points of view that have been established? What keeps it going, and how far can the modern man be an "individual" in it?

In the first place, an association is undoubtedly an "institution" in the current sense. An application to join it and mem-

---

[1] Further details on the legal aspect of the association in Germany may be found in Eugen Sauter, *Der eingetragene Verein. Eine gemeinverständliche Erläuterung des Vereinsrechts unter besonderer Berücksichtigung der neuesten Rechtsprechung* (3d ed.; Munich, 1954).

bership in it draw a hard and fast line between belonging and not belonging to it. The association represents an entity which, as a "legal person," can act as a unified whole in relation to outsiders but also in relation to its members. Its legal registration takes it to a great extent out of the range of any arbitrary action by its members, and so gives it a conditional permanence. This permanent quality is further expressed in the constitution which it has itself adopted as its "law" at the time of its formation and without which it cannot be registered as an association. As the general meeting of the membership is the association's final authority, the affairs of the association must be open to the scrutiny of all the members. There is also reciprocity of services rendered, a necessary concomitant of institutional ties: the constitution of the association establishes the members' rights and duties, which must be suitably adjusted to each other; for breaches of the regulations there are various kinds of conventional penalties. In brief, an association is undoubtedly an institution.

To say this is to repeat the obvious; the statement tells us little. But it becomes very important when we see how far the association is not an institution with unconditional jurisdiction, but one of very limited jurisdiction and effect — in other words, it is an organization. This limitation is made for the benefit of the freedom of the individual person, that is, of the members. Indeed, in Germany the text of the basic law reads to a great extent like a defense of that freedom; and laws enacted subsequently have followed the same course. In this case, the law that provides the legal basis of organizations does actually emerge as a "weapon of the individual."[2] This ensures that both entry and exit are voluntary: there are no "birthright members," and compulsory membership is prohibited; it is entirely at the individual's option whether and for how long he will submit to the constitution of the association. Court rulings have established that the individual has complete freedom in exercising the right to vote; he can be guided in the matter

[2] See Heinrich Mitteis, "Das Recht als Waffe des Individuums," *Die Rechtsidee in der Geschichte* (Weimar, 1957), pp. 514 ff.

entirely by his own personal interests.[3] And since the right to vote is exercised in the general meeting of the membership, which is the association's final authority, the interest of the individual is thereby raised to the status of a basic principle of the association; or at least its priority and inviolability vis-à-vis interests of the association is secured. His obligation toward the association and the other members is also limited, and does not involve the whole of his person. There is no legal prescript from which an obligation of loyalty could be derived. Of course, anyone who continually infringes the association's interests must risk being excluded, but neglect on his part cannot make him liable to legal action.[4] The principle of the absolutely equal treatment of members belongs in this context, too. There is, finally, another thing that has helped to make the association's rules only conditionally binding: high court rulings have established that the constitution of an association is not immutable; the form of the contract between the association and its members must always be open to review — if need be, by a unanimous decision of the general meeting of the membership.[5]

These few features are enough to show that the association is so constituted as to give the individual, *as* an individual, a place at once inside and outside the structure. The organization's bipolar nature, which was discussed earlier, becomes obvious: corporate life is determined both by the institution and, at the same time, by the individual. But whereas in the traditional medieval order of things the institutional aspect predominated, the center of gravity has now just as clearly shifted to the side of the individual; at the same time the institution's claim on man has been appreciably weakened and restricted.

It is true that these legal norms only mark off a framework within which the actual social life is lived. We therefore have to ask further how the associations and federations have actually functioned in the hundred years or so of their existence, always

[3] See Sauter, *op. cit.*, pp. 79–80.
[4] Thus Sauter, *ibid.*, p. 83.
[5] *Ibid.*, p. 38.

keeping before us our chief concerns: What are the forces that make the association function? And what is the position of the individual in relation to the institution? Here we can again distinguish between the two main epochs. While the new society — and with it the world of the associations — was being fashioned, the associations presented, on the whole, quite a different picture from that of our time, a time which continues to build upon foundations that are taken as a matter of course. These periods will be looked at successively with regard to (1) the cohesive forces that held and hold the members together; (2) the relation of the association to other associations; and (3) the question of how the general will is shaped within the association. This will not result in a complete picture, but certain essential factors will stand out. Of course, when one speaks in a generalizing way of "the" association, it must be with great reservations. Many different varieties of the association have always existed side by side. Nonetheless, the main periods of the development stand out quite clearly.

Detachment from "Idealism" and "Community"

The formative period of the new society was marked by a great need to develop community. That is to say, up to the period between the two world wars the pattern followed when persons banded together in association-like groups was determined by what was collective and institutional, by adjustment and deferment of the individual members' own development. And because that is now no longer the case older people like to complain about the decay of group spirit. However, this desire for community, and the willingness to offer devoted service to one's particular community, was produced by historical conditions. We must always remember that the people of the nineteenth century came from a world of all-embracing institutional ties and obligations laid down by a stratified society. And although there was a widespread feeling that the old order was outdated, isolation was a wholly new and untried phenomenon for everyone, and it was by no means regarded as an unmixed blessing. For decades after the abolition of the guilds, the craftsmen demanded their reestablishment, since they saw themselves delivered up alone, defenseless and helpless, to the new world. The peasants, too, were free to manage the plot of ground allotted to them when their feudal obligations and compulsory work in the fields had been abolished; but they too felt the danger to themselves in the new competitive economy, in the "lottery of the produce market," as the advocate of the good old system, Wilhelm Heinrich Riehl, called it.[6] And that is how it was on all sides. The lifting of the old protective orders had given people an unfamiliar and still untested freedom which therefore made them feel an urgent need for some new kind of prop. There could be no return to the old order that embraced all areas of life, and any such hankering finally died away. So the new pattern emerged, giving people more freedom of movement. But, as may be supposed, this new pattern at first emphasized the collective rather than the individual aspect.

Thus the consumer's cooperatives, the labor unions, the political parties, the athletic clubs, the church auxiliaries, the choral societies, the hobby clubs of all kinds, were at first not so much organizations as social communities. Members did not confine themselves to the nominal object of the association, for example, to athletics or to the representation of political interests; they gathered for the sake of conviviality, they held festivals, and they helped each other out. This communal mentality found expression and support in the fact that athletic clubs, cooperative societies, the labor movement, the youth movement, all had their own flag, as well as their own songs in their own songbook. It was customary to wear an association badge or pin even when not engaged in association activities, thus announcing not merely a limited allegiance to the constitution of the association but, instead, a commitment of one's whole person, in striking contrast to the individualist guarantees contained in the constitution. All this was a visible survival of the feeling of interdependence that had been inherited from the institution.

[6] Wilhelm Heinrich Riehl, *Die bürgerliche Gesellschaft* (Stuttgart: Verlag Cotta, 1861), p. 87.

In all this, however, there had to be some compensation for the lapse of the far-reaching cohesive power of the institution and of the actual community of life in village or guild. This compensation took the form of strengthened ties of mind and spirit. Looking back today with distinct aloofness, we like to call them "ideologies," with a distinctly pejorative inflection. In their heyday, however, they used to be referred to as "ideas," and they inspired people's communal activities in the labor movements, the cooperatives, the youth clubs and athletic clubs, which the members served with devoted "idealism." These "ideas" were on various levels; they spoke both to the mind and to the emotions; they demanded reflection and at the same time aroused enthusiasm. Their content was as varied as the forces and aspirations that were then bringing into being the highly differentiated modern world. In part they were animated by class-conscious traditions, particularly in the middle-class organizations of skilled workers or small farmers. The conservative attachment to the past was bound to assume ideological forms, for the simple reason that the old orders had ceased to exist and their effect now had to be derived from forces of the mind and spirit. Or, on the other side, revolutionary or reforming slogans were now put to new uses, for instance, in the labor movement, which aimed at setting in motion a whole new stratum of people, or in the women's movement and the youth movement, which were movements of emancipation that were triggered by the breakup of the "household."

But these movements, whether conservative or revolutionary, were still tied to the old times in one respect: they regarded themselves as "communities," with a "we-consciousness" that allotted the organization a decisive influence on the members' way of life and that therefore did not do full justice either to the nature of the organization or to legal developments. In the area of tension between the institution and the individual, the balance of advantage was still with the institution, though the part that it had to play was now out of harmony with its structure. So there appeared the typical one-sided, even fanatical, ideologies, which the present-day younger "skeptical genera-tion" (Helmut Schelsky)[7] finds barely comprehensible but which the older generation experienced and supported in full. The capacity for one-sidedness probably belongs to a period when a new society, untested and not yet integrated, is being built up. So even the "ideas" are not to be dismissed from the picture of those decades of upheaval and new beginnings; they brought together forces which made it possible to create new structures and which joined people together in common efforts to achieve the aims that beckoned to them.

Today, now that the construction is done with, members are adopting another attitude toward their associations and federa-tions. It is this very outlook which the older people are regret-fully contrasting with the former community consciousness. It may be described as an attitude of individualization and of focusing on the aims of the association [*Versachlichung*]. It turns away from programs that claim to know what the future will bring, and from "ideas," which in fact are now generally called "ideologies." In Germany the devastating confusion of ideas in the Weimar Republic, the excessive and one-sided exploitation of ideological thought by the National Socialists, the universal disillusionment in the collapse of 1945, which gave the lie to any thought of progress, have created a new intellectual situation which has changed life as a whole as well as life within the associations and federations. This develop-ment is taking a similar course in other countries which have experienced either no catastrophes or different or lesser ones.

When one looks at associations today, it is evident that their aims are contracting perceptibly. People go to the club for athletics, or to play chess, or to discuss the cultivation of fruit trees. But conviviality, the holding of festivals, the community spirit, has either weakened or entirely disappeared from asso-ciation life. The members are more intent than ever upon ac-complishing the tasks the association has set itself, often in response to technological advances, and the pursuit of these goals often requires a high degree of competence. But there is

[7] Helmut Schelsky, *Die skeptische Generation* (Düsseldorf: Eugen Die-derichs Verlag, 1957).

not now such a marked feeling of community, and when the evening's activity is over one gets back to the family as quickly as possible, whereas formerly the family would itself be brought along to take an active part in the life of the association. The member's commitment to the association's goals used to be veiled in his commitment to the community espousing them; today it is the goals themselves that matter.

There has been a corresponding weakening of emotional ties. Members no longer get excited, and language that is meant to be moving is regarded as old-fashioned and disturbing. Flags, songs, and other symbols have lost their power. Disenchantment has come to the communal life of the association, which is maintained essentially for utilitarian purposes. In large federations representing particular interests and in cooperative societies, the executive organs are regarded simply as "institutions." One claims their services — advice, legal help, and so on — but looks upon them rather as one looks upon the authorities: as one pays taxes to the latter, so one pays dues to the former, and one expects in return the services of the organization in question.

In a word, life in associations is becoming focused on the aims of the association and receives only a segment of the lives of the members, who no longer dedicate to the association the whole of their persons. The members thus claim the freedom which, by the nature of its structure, the association always offered. So the new development has brought the association's actual life closer to its legal structure; it is more nearly an organization now than it was in the ideological period. For the member, the stress is no longer on the institutional ties, but on the area of individual freedom into which the organization is drawn insofar as it serves that end. In the change that we have described we can see clearly the transition from the former period, when the new society and the associations were in process of formation, to the present period, when that which was established is being consolidated. The associations and federations exist, their existence is taken for granted, and their members no longer have any need to expend much energy or emotion on that score.

From Group Ties to Inclusive Neutrality

The change we have been discussing is also expressed in another way in our associations and federations. By examining this situation, we can explain more clearly the remarkable fact that the partial ties of an institution could formerly bring into its orbit so many aspects of a man's life.

We may take the skilled trades as an illustration. In the period of stratified society, the guild offered a comprehensive way of life. Besides regulating one's occupational life, it also provided a setting for social life. Frequently it represented its members' political interests. In the early period it also amounted to a religious brotherhood. It provided an insurance against sickness and old age. In details the guild varied greatly from place to place, but in principle it was a community that embraced the whole of life.

Intervention by the state, the granting of freedom to conduct a business or pursue an occupation of one's choosing, the breakdown of the "household," and the formation of the new organizations meant that the old guilds were shorn of their diverse responsibilities, many of which now devolved on organizations of the "association" type. Representation of occupational interests fell to trade unions, of political interests to the parties, and of economic interests to the cooperatives. Life insurance went to the insurance companies, religious life to church congregations with their auxiliary societies, social life to such things as choral societies. It seemed to be the complete dismemberment of a self-contained way of life. Yet the dismemberment was by no means as complete as it seemed. For the craftsmen of a town would again and again find themselves together in a network of local associations. Generally speaking, it was frequently the same people who gathered together in the trade union, in the cooperative, in church organizations, in insurance societies, in choral unions, and in the political party. Thus, in practice, this group of people was again ordered along institutional lines and enjoyed institutional benefits — people knew each other and shared the same general outlook, and there was again formed a comprehensive pattern of life, although it was of an open kind. It mattered little whether the individual craftsman turned with his particular skills and interests more to the work of the union, the cooperative, the church, or the political party. The people involved were the same from one association to the next, or at least were much alike, and so the individual could feel that his whole person was bound up with the place where his own interests lay.

There was now much interlocking of this kind in the world of associations, though, of course, there was a good deal of overlapping. Indeed, the interlocking was very carefully planned. In Germany, for example, a class-conscious laborer could represent his political interests in the Social Democratic party, could join one of the trade unions for his occupational interests, a consumers' cooperative as a consumer, a free-thinkers' organization for philosophical orientation, a workers' choral union for social life, and a workers' athletic club for sports. Like the middle-class craftsmen, the workers had here a comprehensive institutional system which every single member could use to the full, even if he did not at a particular time belong to all the associations in question. For the Roman Catholic laborer there were the Center Party, the Catholic workers' movement, the Christian trade unions, and "Cologne" consumers' cooperatives, all of which brought a goodly number of people together at the local level as well. Some of the people in these groups also met in other federations with Protestants and in still others with persons belonging to different social strata. There were similarly organized associations of small farmers in rural areas, and middle-class citizens would often have their local group of associations where the members could meet freely.

There remain traces, but only traces, of this kind of harmonious and homogeneous communal life. We feel today that the formation of associations and federations according to class and status is essentially outmoded, because those old concepts of class have become open to question and the old dividing lines between social strata very fluid. A "workers' athletic club" is today a relic of bygone times. The tendency is now more and more for a church society to be classless and politically neutral, for the cultural association to be neither political nor religious, and for the political club to be open to people of all classes and creeds.

The large federations reconstituted in Germany after World War II have taken all this into account. They have done away with the old fragmentation, and have turned themselves into inclusive federations, for fragmentation was what the old interlocking, "network" system had produced: since the individual member of the association was required to possess an increasing number of membership qualifications, the associations remained small and therefore capable of accomplishing but little. When the German Farmers' Federation was reconstituted, therefore, it was as a unified organization representing the whole of West German agriculture, whereas before 1933 the small farmers, the tenant farmers, and the big landed proprietors had all been organized separately. The development has been plain, too, in the reorganization of the labor unions. The German Federation of Labor Unions, with its sixteen modern industrial unions, aims at providing a broad and politically neutral representation of all employees. It has replaced a great mass of labor unions, large, small, and tiny, each with its own bias of class, geographical region, politics, and world view. The reorganization of consumers' cooperatives, athletic clubs, and so on, has taken a similar course. Even the political parties either have shed, or are trying to shed, their identification with certain social groups. Thus the organizational development itself exhibits the increasing concentration on the limited objectives of the particular federation. Today, therefore, it would be difficult to lose oneself in devotion to an association or a federation. For some decades after their old institutions had disintegrated, the old classes found a substitute in the association "networks"; for the new working "class" the latter actually provided the very kind of institution that aroused and kept alive their class consciousness. With the transition from the association networks to the neutral, inclusive federations, classes and the vestiges of classes lost the institutional structure they held dear, and that structure dissolved because class consciousness and status consciousness dwindled. Thus, as the association developed, the structures of the old stratified society gave place to equality of rights for everyone. Social reality caught up with the development of the law.

The Shift in Decision-Making

A central question for every institution, and therefore for the association, is that of decision-making. Where and how are decisions made about the life of the association, where and how is its course directed, both in everyday matters and in crises? According to the plan and legal structure of the association, its decisions are made through a consensus between the members as a whole and the executive committee or governing board elected at the general meeting of the membership. The ultimate authority is the general meeting, through which the executive board is elected and charged with its responsibilities. Once that is done, however, the meeting cannot take upon itself to deal at will with any of the association's affairs that are, according to the constitution, within the jurisdiction of the executive board. On the other hand, the general meeting can withdraw its confidence from the board and remove it from office. The relationship is therefore a permanent two-sided one, founded on confidence. The legal framework of the association leaves open the question where the balance falls in any particular case: whether the governing board is only an executive instrument under the active direction of the members, or whether it is to have the initiative. In the latter case the question is again left open whether one dominating personality at the top is to guide the association's destinies as its chairman, or whether the members of the executive board act and decide as a whole. In any case there must necessarily be a two-sided relationship resting on confidence and mutual understanding. If that is lacking, the association degenerates into either an amorphous clique or the servile henchmen of an autocrat or autocratic group. In either case it is no longer an association or organization.

The development that witnessed the recession of the members' ideological interests into the background in favor of a focus on utilitarian goals also resulted, in the case of most associations and federations, in a transfer of much of the decision-making power to the executive board. It is true that even in the ideological period the tone was often set by a powerful group, or even by one outstanding personality, but when these leaders rallied the members round an "idea" they could count on a ready and self-sacrificing response, which in turn gave them support and encouragement. Thus there was between leadership and membership a dynamic relationship of action and interaction.

Today this interaction is often lacking. In our time, voting for the governing board generally runs a very prosaic course. The members, if in fact they turn up at all, are glad if they can find a few competent people who are willing to be placed on the slate, or if the old board is willing to remain in office. In such cases the secret ballot is generally dispensed with; indeed, the voting may well be by keeping silent: "Anyone opposed, please raise your hand." In that case, there is not even any active sign of approval. If the balloting is to produce a large turnout and keen interest in the results, there has to be some especially weighty business at hand.

But there is another important reason for the lack of candidates and for people's readiness to keep the trusted members of a governing board in office: even the smaller associations, and still more the bigger ones, are today faced with problems with which not every member is necessarily able to cope. Therefore to fill adequately the post of a board member, and still more that of the chairman, one needs a good deal of knowledge, experience, tact, and energy. Federations representing special interests, cooperatives, and even athletic clubs and church organizations are much more difficult to direct today than they used to be, since the field of responsibilities has greatly extended, and special knowledge is urgently needed everywhere. And it is in the achievement of its aims that the association stands or falls.

It will be seen, then, that a very large measure of responsibility for the stability of the association falls on the executive board. Whereas formerly the association's mainstay was the members' community consciousness, which also supported the governing board's initiative, today the strength needed to give the association stability and make it flourish comes from the personal aptitude and efficiency of the board. The association is dependent on that.

This structure implies, however, that aptitude and efficiency of a special kind are needed. For the entity is still an association, and that means that the general meeting of the membership keeps its guaranteed rights. Any member can take the initiative at any time, whether at an ordinary general meeting or by calling a special meeting. Then, if the matter is pushed through, the meeting can pass a vote of no confidence in the executive board. The board is therefore dependent on that confidence, which means it must remain on terms of mutual understanding with the members. The executive board of an association cannot make decisions in isolation; it must listen to the members and be able to convince them. In addition, however, the range of present-day tasks demands something that is in any case generally required by the association's constitution: consensus within the executive board. The board's responsibility is therefore not one to be exercised in isolation; time and again it is a matter for discussion, in which and out of which the decisions are shaped. That, at least, is what the circumstances demand; whether it is what happens in practice is another matter.

But all this still leaves untouched one very important development in the world of the association, namely, the growing importance of the full-time official. Everything that we have so far been discussing is in the setting of what might be called voluntary associations; but our big organizations are tending more and more to become officials' associations. What does that imply?

In these an organ of the association, one which is not even provided for in the original legal structure, is beginning to determine the character of the association as a whole. The conduct of affairs is generally a matter for the executive board; but if the affairs increase so much that they can no longer be handled on a part-time basis, they are handed over to a full-time manager; and if he is given a staff, a new organization arises within the association.

The same development that made the executive board predominant in the association — namely, the complication of duties — has therefore in many cases shifted the balance again, this time beyond the board to the trained permanent staff, to the "officials." The result is simply that the unpaid members of the executive board, despite their devotion and long experience, have to rely on the advice of their expert staff. That means that, in point of fact, the power to make decisions has in numerous cases been transferred to that quarter, without its being recognized in the constitution of the association. There are actually federations that are managed — and not badly managed — by officials whose authority is not derived from the constitution any more than it is in the case of association law. In such cases, where the actual management is by officials, they are the people whose skill and efficiency determine the life and stability of the federation.

Even so, the federation is still an association according to association law, and the staff gets its authority, via the executive board, from the members. That is how it is legitimized, and its entire setup makes it dependent — as is the executive board — on the confidence of the members. The staff will, in the nature of the case, listen to the members, inform them, and convince them, and it will remain in close touch with the executive board and with other unpaid elected bodies.

Thus the same thing holds good for the paid officials as for the executive board, namely that the federation is carried along by a very personal individual responsibility. In view of the federation's structure, however, this individual responsibility is not the same as the power to make arbitrary decisions. On the contrary, those who bear the responsibility must keep in touch with various quarters and must make the decisions issue from the resulting discussions.

6

The Development of

the Business

Strict Hierarchy as the Early Pattern

A "business," like an association, is an "organization," a point that now needs no further elaboration. It is enough to recall here that the "business" did not appear on the scene till the worker ceased to be included in the life and community of the "household" and instead became a party to a "free contract of employment," which merely put him under obligation to work according to his own special skill and left him otherwise free. In that way the "journeyman" or the farm laborer, who was tied down by the old system of rank and class, was superseded by the "employee." This limitation of the authority of the institution and of its claims on the person is an essential characteristic of a developed organization. With it there appeared the further characteristics of the organization, namely, secularization and flexibility. From its origin, the business has been a secular affair; there have been no sacrosanct businesses. What first induced the entrepreneur to choose this new structure was the possibility it offered of ready accommodation to the new conditions of production and marketing. So when we ask about the forces that make the business function, and about the individual's position in it, we are still dealing with the subject, "man and the organization."

Today there are businesses of all sizes, from small enterprises employing a few craftsmen to the smelter or steel mill with labor forces of ten thousand or more people. We are now so familiar with the idea of an "industrial" society that we are apt to overestimate the part that industry has in the total labor picture, and then to identify it in the main with basic industry. Actually, in 1956 barely two fifths of the employees in the Federal Republic of Germany were employed in industry, and of these only one half were in businesses that employed five hundred or more; only one employee in five worked in basic industry. There were just about as many people working in businesses employing craftsmen as in basic industry. It is obvious that, according to these figures, the term "industrial society" is inappropriate.

If we judge by the actual importance of industry, however, the term is much more justified. We are not referring here to the economic and technical aspect. The important thing in our context is that industry has to a great extent become the accepted standard for the organization of a business, for the place men have in it, the way they are related to it, and the expectations they bring to it. That is true particularly of basic industry. In the pages that follow, therefore, it is not only the requirements of simplification but the subject itself that justify the focusing of our attention primarily on the large industrial concern.

What were the forces that underlay the functioning of the industrial concern during the first few decades after its inception? What was the connecting link between the people who worked together here in a system of production that was as yet undeveloped and untested? What was it that ensured the co-operation of all the parts for the desired end? To put it briefly, it was the hierarchy, headed by the entrepreneur and rigidly adhering to the principle of command and obedience. This hierarchy was the exact antipode of the association with its decisions moving upward from below.

In our historical survey in chapter three we pointed out that the modern business, as a new kind of social structure, was created by the entrepreneur. As an individual person who had shaken off the old traditional institutional ties, he recruited the workers, also as individuals, from their "households" and other restrictive influences, and built up the business according to his own desires and plans. So it was natural that at first all the threads of the organization started from him and returned to him. The business was a pyramid with a single apex, and the vital fact was the vertical lines of communication from the entrepreneur, via the intermediate authority of supervisors and foremen, to the mass of the workers who carried out the tasks. Every member of the labor force had his place on a particular vertical line of communication. He received instructions and supervision from the next higher authority. The only method of communication with someone else working at his own level was through their common immediate superior.

As the labor force grew and the clerical staff expanded to significant proportions, the development of the latter at first continued along the same lines. The entrepreneur was always able to fall back on the model of the absolutist state, which had earlier created the hierarchical organization of the civil service and the army, both of which likewise culminated in a single apex.

The results achieved by this early form of business organization were significant. It was here that a new social structure was first created and developed to a considerable degree of efficiency. It was here that the basis of modern mechanized production was laid. And here — an achievement that is now generally overlooked — the working man was taken out of the traditional category of household craftsman and was disciplined and trained in the conditions of modern employment. It is easy today to underestimate the transformation that this entailed and the compulsion to which a man had to be subjected so that he should learn to do continuous and uniform work by the clock, regimented among a great number of fellow workmen, with the special kind of exactitude that the machine requires. The necessary compulsion was exercised, in the early industrial period, by an unrestricted hierarchy.

But this unilateral hierarchy of early industrial business was an early form of organization that was bound to be only a transitional affair. In Germany it arose in the nineteenth century — in England, even earlier — simultaneously with the new legal code that gave every law-abiding citizen equal standing under the law. At the same time there was a growing demand that this equal standing should be made a political and social reality. In that context, such unilateral subordination was not to be tolerated in the long run. In other words, during long decades, and under the pressure of forces that were now liberated, business life developed into an organization in the full sense of the word. The early unilateral hierarchy was not that.

This can be seen clearly in the various sentiments with which the entrepreneurs of the time expressed themselves with regard to their position at the summit of the business hierarchy. According to L. H. A. Geck[1] we can distinguish four types.

1) The "libertarian-legal" entrepreneur sought to divest the relationship between employers and employees of all ethical considerations and public responsibilities. The new free contract of employment was understood as a rational exchange of a specific amount of work for a specific wage, and beyond that neither side was to be under any obligations or further commitments. This "libertarian-legal" attitude was an attempt to interpret the new principle of organization in a purely rational way, with man brazenly regarded simply as a means to an end. Later development has shown that this concept of organization, while it regarded itself as purely "objective," was actually lacking in objectivity because it ran contrary not only to ethical demands but also to business aims. A business structure, even of a hierarchical kind, cannot in the long run be maintained on such a basis.

[1] L. H. A. Geck, *Die sozialen Arbeitsverhältnisse im Wandel der Zeit. Eine geschichtliche Einführung in die Betriebssoziologie* ("Schriftenreihe des Instituts für Betriebssoziologie und soziale Betriebslehre an der Technischen Hochschule zu Berlin," 1 [Berlin: Springer-Verlag, 1931]).

2) A widespread development in the direction of "social right"[2] did away long ago with the narrow legalistic view taken in the "libertarian-legal" position. The latter was at one time written into the German Civil Code. But since then legislation and judicial decisions have worked to "change the formal ethic of freedom back into a material ethic of social responsibility." They have again (although in a new fashion) recognized a contract as a social matter from which "may stem a range of duties required of both parties and going far beyond the actual terms agreed on" in the contract.[3] Thus legal theory and practice have been compelled by practical necessities to work in the direction of overcoming the purely rational idea of organization, and the actual development in business life has followed suit.

3) The "libertarian-humanitarian," personal conception of the entrepreneur's role also proved to be a transitional one and, ultimately, untenable. It kept itself aloof, to be sure, from the brazen irresponsibility of the first type, and it took into account the need to treat the workers well, to improve their wages, and to adopt an enlightened social policy within the business. But its basis was still solely the goodwill of the entrepreneur and his feeling of personal responsibility. This attitude, too, remained a unilateral one and thus no longer accorded with the new legal and moral bases of the social order.

4) Another widespread attitude, which was just as unilateral and, therefore, untenable, savored most strongly of traditional patterns. It was that of the patriarchal entrepreneur. It too was prompted by a feeling of concern and responsibility for the worker, but its underlying principle was: "Everything *for* the worker; nothing *through* him." This was an echo of the social pattern of the "household," which had linked master and servants in a regime that embraced them all. But that regime was no longer in existence, and so this attitude, too, had

---

[2] See Franz Wieacker, *Das Sozialmodell der klassischen Privatrechtsgesetzbücher und die Entwicklung der modernen Gesellschaft* (Karlsruhe, 1953), p. 21.
[3] *Ibid.*, pp. 18–19.

no real foundation on which to stand. An old-style master of the house had legal rights over his household, and was the sole representative of their rights and interests. In a society where every adult had acquired his own legal rights, no such tutelage was possible.

All four of these legal conceptions and attitudes corresponded to the structural pattern of the unilateral business hierarchy based on command and obedience. They provided its justification and rationale. Like them, however, the unilateral business hierarchy proved in the long run to be untenable. As time went on, it grew less and less able to meet practical requirements, and so the early entrepreneurs' conceptions of their roles, along with the early business structures, faced a crisis. It has been seen for a long time that they are giving way to a new attitude and new structures. In accord with our general purposes, we can and should discuss here only those elements indicative of the growing need of personal responsibility that is observable in this development.

The Individualizing of Jobs and the Growth of Personal Responsibility

A process of increasing significance is the general decrease in assembly-line work. By that term we mean the simultaneous performance of work of the same or a similar nature by long rows of male or female workers under immediate supervision. Everyone does only one thing, carrying out only a very simple part of the total enterprise, a part that he can be taught quite quickly, so that he can easily be replaced by another worker. Work of this kind is planned so that a great number of people are brought into one factory, and the amount that can be produced by each individual is increased by a systematic "division of labor." The classical description and theoretical basis of this method was given by Adam Smith in his famous account of the pin factory.[4]

This kind of assembly line in manufacturing existed as early as the eighteenth century, when fabrics, porcelain, or guns for

[4] Adam Smith, *The Wealth of Nations* (1776), Bk. I, chap. 1.

the needs of the absolutist state were methodically produced in big rooms. Early industrial production in the nineteenth century began by adopting a very similar pattern, and so it had little difficulty in absorbing the masses of unskilled workers who flocked to the towns. On the landed estates there was the corresponding "column of reapers," and — if we may be allowed a sidelong glance — the military tactics of the time produced the same kind of picture in the long lines of infantry advancing or firing.

At first the spread of mechanization produced no change in the picture. The same principle of the assembly line was applied, for example, in the "rationalization" that intensified industrial production in Germany from about 1925 to 1928 by use of conveyor belts on production lines and by extensive workings in the coal mines. The increased clerical staffs of that day were often placed in large one-room offices, again to perform the same kind of work on a large scale under supervision. Today, however, industry is more and more emerging from this stage. This change has not come by way of any sharp break; it has involved rather a transition, which began early in some branches of manufacturing, is at present proceeding only slowly in others, and can never be entirely completed. Industry will always have to require a certain amount of monotonous assembly-line work. But it makes a difference whether that kind of work predominates, or whether a different kind of work is representative of the picture as a whole.

"The individual workman is no longer interchangeable at will. He is an individuality, and he is treated as far as possible individually, for one has to rely on his doing of his own accord, at his own particular job, everything that is expected of him . . . . Technological progress has gradually created more and more jobs in which the worker is able to do responsible and not uninteresting work in comparative freedom." Thus reads a recent sociological study made in industry by Hans Paul Bahrdt.[5] These facts take some time to become widely known, and up to now they have been overlooked by many,

[5] Hans Paul Bahrdt, *Industriebürokratie* (Stuttgart, 1958), p. 35.

especially in analyses and critiques of Western culture. But the conclusions that Bahrdt has reached are the result of long-term investigations, and anyone conversant with the facts will confirm them. Of course, they are not to be understood as rigidly applicable to all the jobs in industry today, but as indicating the direction of a development: "Technological progress has gradually created more and more jobs in which the worker . . . ."

Even without systematic investigations, the careful observer today will notice the continually increasing diversification in the world of work. Without special training, however, it has become impossible to obtain an overall picture of the great variety of occupations and branches of work today — a fact that makes job counseling and choice of a career extremely difficult. In the Federal Republic today there are something approaching twenty thousand different occupational designations, with the number still on the increase. And even the same designation can denote a variety of specific jobs, depending on the particular business and on the changes in duties that may accompany changes within the business.

Moreover, it will not escape the careful observer that not only are our occupations becoming increasingly diversified all the time, but the required qualifications are also being steadily raised. In the early days of industry, say in 1880, a young man from the country, after completing his military service, would have no difficulty in entering a factory and meeting its requirements without undergoing an apprenticeship. A short period of instruction was all that was needed for carrying out the simple manufacturing processes of the time. Today there is a growing number of industrial jobs for which apprenticeship has become essential. The need is met to a considerable extent through recourse to apprentices in the skilled trades, but industry has also adopted the practice of training its own. Careers in industrial production have become careers for which training is needed, and the qualifications demanded of the would-be entrant are becoming higher and higher.

In this connection there is a particularly interesting development going on in the upper echelons of skilled work. There are occupations, or perhaps one should say activities, for which a very specialized familiarity with the work involved has to be acquired, and in which a really solid efficiency can be produced only by long years of experience. For jobs of this particular kind it is difficult, if not impossible, to provide training that really meets the requirements. They remain "skilled occupations," but of a new kind, for they draw together people of the most varied background and education, who have a special aptitude and inclination for the work in question. Among these are, for example, people who work at programming and tabulating with modern office machines or who operate computers. The impossibility of any standardized training for these activities — we cannot go into the reasons here — is an indication of the high degree of individualization that has taken place in modern work processes, for an apprenticeship is the institutionalizing of occupational training. When work of the kind needed at the very apex of technological development eludes such institutionalization, that is a very significant sign of the new trend in technical work. This belongs to our second period of industrialization, and contradicts the experiences that accumulated in the first period. That is why it is so slow to sink into people's minds, and why we still hear loud complaints, which were justified seventy years ago, that technological progress is eliminating skilled work.

Here we can do no more than briefly indicate the striking connection between technological progress and the occupational diversification and higher performance standards that follow as a result. It should be noted, however, that the result of the division of labor has not been simply to break down existing patterns of work. It was only in the early days that the various stages of work to be performed at the bench or in the office were allocated to different workers so as to raise the individual output. This splitting-up of work made it possible to institute much more complicated procedures in the production process as a whole. This in turn meant at first that the direction and coordination of the individual processes required more skill and versatility, while the actual doing of the work continued to follow the monotonous assembly-line pattern that we have mentioned above. Now, in the process of mechanization, the machine proceeded to take over the monotonous working processes one by one. In a certain sense the people who had been employed to carry out these monotonous processes provided the models for the machines which soon took over these processes and were able to do them faster and more accurately. This meant that for many people in the lower positions there now remained only the more complicated tasks of constructing, directing, and controlling the machines. The mechanization of working processes left fewer and fewer places that the machine could not, or could not yet, take over. The worker at a mechanical lathe now occupied — though in a different way — the position previously held by the foreman at the head of a whole roomful of handworkers in a factory.

Present-day technological progress is taking a (provisionally) final step in this development, in the automation that is the subject of so much discussion. Automation means that even very complicated problems of control and direction ("the controlling of control") are taken over by the machine, and that the only part left for men to play is that of ultimate supervision and repairs. At the same time, the possibilities of automation are generally overestimated. Careful estimates have shown that in the United States in the next twenty years not more than from ten to twenty percent of the employees will be directly affected by it, and that the figure in the Federal Republic of Germany will probably be lower. Thus it seems likely that, as regards future production and office work, we can count on a mixed bag of work processes — automated, wholly or partly mechanized, and nontechnical.[6] So we must not assume that assembly-line work is going to be completely eliminated by highly technical work performed on an individual basis. What is important is that the present course of the development is moving not in the direction of widespread extension of assembly-line work, but toward a diminution of it.

[6] *Ibid.,* p. 68.

What has been said allows us to draw important conclusions in answer to our questions about the place of man in the organization, about the forces that make the organization function, and about the nature of "individualization." Work is carried out in businesses, that is, in organizations. However, the most essential characteristic of an organization is often taken to be its rationality, that is, its openness to calculation in terms of specific services exchanged for a specific equivalent. The extreme libertarianism of the nineteenth century believed it possible to calculate precisely by the clock or by the piece the work that was done, and to give a full equivalent for that work by paying a wage that was calculated with equal precision. Even today that view is still held by many, but it no longer fits the facts. For if one can give it some rough justification when it is applied to monotonous and uniform assembly-line work (it cannot be entirely justified for any human work), in skilled, responsible work that is checked by the worker himself, something more is contributed — something which is no longer calculable and which cannot be given a monetary value. Today, however, this "more" of personal qualification and responsibility is no longer confined to the positions of leadership at the summit, but has penetrated deep into the mass of the workers themselves. Experience, know-how, careful work, a sense of responsibility, devotion to the task — all very personal qualities — are needed today in every stratum of industry. And the more urgent and the more general the demand for them, the more the success of the business as a whole depends on them. This does not diminish the importance of a well-conceived and well-planned organizational structure. But as more skilled individual responsibility is needed, the organizational scheme will give it free play, and not stifle it with an excess of institutional controls and regulations.

The Work Group

Besides the worker's relationship to his work, his relationship to his fellow workers is also important for the success of the business organization. This relationship, too, has been greatly changed by the technological development just described.

The importance of this relationship for the business was not recognized in the early days. It was only in the twentieth century that it was, as one might say, "discovered" and made generally known.

In the early days of manufacturing and industry, that is, when assembly-line work predominated, industrial organization consisted almost exclusively in the transmission of orders from the top downward; regulations were passed down through the chain of command, and supervision of the workers was ensured. The business looked on its workers as isolated individuals. Naturally they had ties among themselves through kinship or friendship, but these ties appeared as of no significance for the business; the organization had nothing to do with them.

Then, in the first half of the twentieth century, sociological studies in industry discovered the "informal group" as a factor which not only arises and exists side by side with others but also has an appreciable influence on the workers' productivity. Of these researches, the best known are those by the American sociologist Elton Mayo, who hit upon this fact in his well-known "Hawthorne experiment" at Western Electric and published clear and cogent reports on it.[7] He exploded the "rabble hypothesis," according to which the workers are a "rabble" of individuals governed by selfish material motives;[8] and he made it possible for people generally to realize that work in industry is always a group activity. A great variety of factors lead to the formation of "informal groups" in a business. The latter determine, not only the working rhythm of their members, but their general evaluation of the atmosphere within the company, their feeling of security, the pattern of their social relationships, and their efficiency and productivity.[9]

[7] See the summary (with bibliography) of the Hawthorne experiment in Elton Mayo's *The Social Problems of an Industrial Civilization* (Boston: Harvard University Graduate School of Business Administration, Division of Research, 1945), pp. 68–86.
[8] *Ibid.*, pp. 34–58.
[9] See R. Dahrendorf, *Industrie- und Betriebssoziologie* (Berlin, 1956).

The creation and the modus operandi of informal groups cannot be arranged at will, but at the same time such groups are unavoidable and indispensable for the life of the business organization. Here we are again brought up against the fact that there is more to an organization than simply rational planning and compulsion; here too there is a vital "extra" without which the organization cannot function and endure, but which is a part of it and must therefore be included in the concept "organization." Ideally, any such informal group would coincide with a formal one, that is, with one set up by the business organization itself. In that case, the formal group would itself be a well-rounded and efficient little organization.

But all this does not yet take account of the state of affairs corresponding to advanced mechanization. The informal group is still an "order," a community, which uses the typical institutional pattern to direct its members' conduct: public scrutiny, reciprocal surveillance, collective sanctions, demarcation from those outside, and so on. But here too the march of technological progress is putting personal relationships in the place of the institutional collective pattern.

This process has recently been the subject of a thorough sociological study at a steel mill.[10] The authors of the study have chosen to call the older and the newer types of cooperation between fellow workers "team cooperation" and "structural cooperation," respectively. What was discovered and described here in regard to concrete individual working processes in a basic industry is of much more general importance for the structure of human relationships as they are affected by a highly refined technology.

The working conditions under which one finds "team cooperation" are comparatively simple. A small group of fellow workers is faced with a common task, which must be finished in a specified time. Within this framework everyone has his own particular task, but in its fulfillment he is given a certain

[10] Heinrich Popitz, H. P. Bahrdt, E. A. Jüres, and H. Kesting, *Technik und Industriearbeit. Soziologische Untersuchungen in der Hüttenindustrie* (Tübingen, 1957).

amount of latitude. There is some freedom with regard to the use of time, and personal dexterity and experience may make things easier and save time and energy. The individuals who are working together can also move about in comparative freedom, instead of being tied down to one spot. All this makes it possible for the members of the group to help each other; by joint effort they can overcome any breakdowns or difficulties or overloadings that crop up, and they can help to pull a beginner or a weaker member of the team along. This willingness to give mutual help arises in the first place from a moral constraint: anyone can expect help only as long as he is ready to give help himself. But comradeship may go beyond that, simply through the human solidarity that is "informally" developed and cultivated in the group. "Team cooperation" is the kind of working comradeship that might appear from time immemorial in all primitive or only slightly mechanized communal work. Our point in describing it is that it provides a background against which we can distinguish more sharply the pattern of cooperative work under highly technical conditions: "structural cooperation."

This "structural cooperation" is a concomitant of today's complicated technical apparatuses. It does not allow the direct, shoulder-to-shoulder kind of work found in team cooperation, the personal coming-to-lend-a-hand in case of need. Each of one's fellow workers is tied down to his fixed place in the whole apparatus, and cooperation is made possible only by a complicated technical system.

We may take as a well-known and very common example (one offered in the work just cited) the individual driver in street traffic. The phenomena here are very much the same as in highly mechanized production processes: the actions of one of the parties concerned are related to the actions of all the others — "Everyone does what he must do, so that another can do what he has to do."[11] For this there are, indeed, fixed rules, but there is no permanently fixed pattern. In the course of the successive happenings there is an almost unlimited combination of possibilities and variations. And alongside the

[11] *Ibid.*, p. 61.

110

comparatively narrow margin of choice allowed (which is like that in work that is not, or not highly, mechanized) there arises, again and again, the necessity to make decisions at great risk.

This becomes particularly urgent in the case of a tie-up or a breakdown of any sort: one variation brings in its wake others that have to be improvised. It is here that the possibility of mutual assistance is also given: by skillful improvisation one person may intercept another's mistake and correct it indirectly. The margin for this is generally only slight, but it is very important. Seconds and millimeters may make all the difference.

The general significance of these observations, reaching far beyond the industrial process, is seen and recorded in the study we have been discussing, and we wish to quote a few of its conclusions: "Structural cooperation, therefore, creates its own atmosphere, the effects and concomitants of which can be generally observed in the 'industrial society': joint action is possible without any personal commitment. At the same time, however, there emerges an unusual intensity of interdependence, which presupposes mutual trust and a levelheaded trustworthiness on the part of each individual in his particular contribution to the effort as a whole. As soon as one falls short of the necessary minimum of specific technical competence demanded by the situation, this is 'unsocial' behavior. But above this lower limit there emerges a kind of mutual appreciation . . . ."[12]

These words state with unusual conciseness a number of very important things about man's personal existence in modern society. There is, first, the statement about the "unusual intensity of interdependence," which is of very general validity and can be paired, paradoxically, with the observation that such interdependence is possible "without any personal commitment." This is a quite new kind of social detachment, of which we read more in still another passage: "This detailed, exacting, and fatiguing dependence at the same time leaves in an unusual kind of detachment from one another the people

[12] *Ibid.*, p. 188.

who have become dependent on each other."[13] This detachment, however, is again made good by a specific kind of trust, namely, a trust in a person's ability to do his job and in his ability to cope with critical situations. As we shall see later, this need for trust in the other person's concern with the issue or task at hand is a vital element in the personal life of people today. And the justification for such trust is rightly described by the authors as the basis of a "social" attitude: to disappoint the trust is to show an "unsocial" attitude. To understand this, we have to remember that coping with the task that constitutes one's particular contribution to the effort as a whole does not mean applying only part of one's personality; on the contrary, the whole person is involved in the effort. In his analysis of the demands of jobs of any degree of technicality, Popitz states that "every human response to the challenge of a particular situation contains a 'more' factor." The workers "relate their particular part in the whole effort to their persons, and their response issues from the whole context of their lives, their capacities, and their energies, and it is therefore sometimes more than is asked of them."[14]

Thus by looking at the pattern of jointly executed work employing highly technical equipment and processes we have been able to add other important details to help us to answer our questions: What is it that makes modern "organized" society function? And what are we to understand by the "individualizing" of man in that society? In "structural cooperation" we see a man who is very much "individualized," yet who represents, not an isolated individual, but one who is united to others in a new and very specific way — detached and yet closely united, and, indeed, united in concern for the task at hand.

The Changed Function of Those in Authority

The developments that we have described have not been without effect on the significance and shape of the business hierarchy. Of course, the hierarchy continues to exist, and is

[13] *Ibid.*, p. 187.
[14] *Ibid.*, pp. 176–77.

always bound to do so. But the tasks of the men in authority, at their various levels, have greatly changed. This is particularly obvious in the case of the foreman.

"We notice in many places that the foreman is regularly pushed out of the normal working process in which he used to take an active part by apportioning work, giving orders, checking on what has been done, and correcting. There is hardly any place now for 'directions' from the foreman. The worker himself knows what is to be done; it can be inferred from the conditions imposed by the technical equipment. His method of doing it is checked by automatic recording instruments, or else it need not be checked at all, for any mistake would lead to an obvious disruption of the work. For advice and instruction there is little opportunity, except during the period of training. Quite often the worker understands his particular job better than the foreman does, as the latter has in the meantime taken over quite different tasks."[15]

This process of change in the old functions of those in authority was noticed long ago, and is spoken of as the foreman crisis. It may be regarded as symptomatic of the general development, a development running parallel with technological progress. The more highly technical the work is, the more individualized are the jobs (contrary to what is generally supposed), and the greater are the demands on the workers' sense of responsibility and their capacity for supervision of their own work. And in the same measure the importance of the hierarchy in the day-to-day work, as supervisors and transmitters of instructions, is reduced.

But, once again, the matter does not rest there, with an individualizing that isolates. The crisis of the hierarchy consists not only in a growing feeling of responsibility, but also in a growing importance of the horizontal, or lateral, ties between workers in business. This, too, has been pointed out by Bahrdt in the book we have cited several times. He describes a transition that actually took place from a hierarchical to a cooperative system.[16] When working procedures are divided up and the

[15] Bahrdt, *op. cit.*, pp. 29–30.
[16] *Ibid.*, pp. 62 ff,

individual processes apportioned to various departments, the latter are obliged to cooperate with each other directly. To make a detour via the common immediate superior wastes time and is inefficient. This means, however, that increased, indeed vital, importance attaches to a form of connecting tie between workers that was unknown to the old vertical hierarchy. Responsibility for the cooperation of the various departments is shared, not only by departmental heads and foremen, but also by individual workers. That means a further extension of personal responsibility at every level of the business.

What this responsibility does is to put the individual at the point of intersection of numerous vertical and horizontal connecting lines, all of which are important for the accomplishment of the work. His responsibility at this point of intersection is one of independence, but not of isolation. The conduct of a business in the present day, therefore, does not mean the enforcement of the will of those on top, but the coordination of many very diverse centers of responsibility. It means, if it is done properly, that the individual responsibility demanded by the facts of the case is given adequate scope and is assured of its right place in the whole context.

The course of this development pushes the old concepts of command, obedience, and supervision into the background, and the relation of those in authority to their subordinates acquires a dimension of freedom in which one responsible person talks to another, with both intent on the issues. The subordinate becomes at the same time a co-worker.

In this connection we may quote Bahrdt once more: "The stress on the relationship of superior to subordinate is changed; one might also say that one of the primal forms of authority is restored. In a form of dialogue that focuses on the issues and employs the kind of colloquial speech used between colleagues, there emerges on occasion an esoteric teacher-pupil relationship. Of course, the superior has to apportion the work assignments. But there is no point in turning this duty into a command. On the contrary, the particular assignment must be explained in conversation. If it is understood, and if all doubts and obscurities are removed, there is no longer any need for commands: the task speaks for itself. It can be accomplished in that way, and in no other."[17]

We must now add another very important development, which in some degree reflects that which we observed in the federation. There, in principle, legitimation and decision-making came in the first place from the membership as a whole, but the emergence of a full-time staff meant the introduction of a hierarchy, which intersects and merges with the original structure in a peculiar way. In the business, all the authority proceeded, and proceeds, in principle, from the summit; but now the opposite principle has come in to cut across it. In Germany the shop committees, which had in many cases come into being as a practical necessity even before the First World War, have since 1920 been legally constituted councils, an established component of all businesses or companies with twenty or more employees; in smaller establishments there is an elected shop steward. In the Federal Republic the law in effect since 1952 states that "employer and shop committee shall work together in mutual confidence . . . for the welfare of the business and its employees" in all matters that concern the personal position of the employee in the business.[18]

Thus there has been introduced here, both in law and in the actual structure of the business, an element of self-determination and self-government that once again marks a significant breaking away from the former unilateral hierarchy.

In conclusion, we shall cast a glance at the situation at the summit of the business. With such far-reaching changes in the structure over which it presides, management itself cannot have remained entirely unchanged. Many of the changes that it has undergone may perhaps be understood in the following way. The position of the entrepreneur who created and developed the business was from the very beginning quite free of institutional ties and supports, and required that he should have a very independent personality. The recent development has

[17] *Ibid.*, pp. 98–99.
[18] *Betriebsverfassungsgesetz* (1952), par. 49.

extended and intensified these demands on the personality of the people occupying the top positions. When we see what such positions demand of their holders, we get a very good idea of what personal responsibility means in modern society.

From the very beginning, the entrepreneur could be an entrepreneur only when he was free from the traditional regulations of the guilds and from other ties of the stratified society of his day. Only in that way could he develop the creative initiative needed for devising and testing the new methods of production. To do this, indeed, he had to break through not only guild and status but also, very often, the traditional occupational categories. The longer the development continued, the more the entrepreneur's achievement became one that was freed from the confinements of these traditional categories.

There remained one institution, however, to which his achievements were at first firmly tied: property. It was by his ownership of the means of production that he justified the extraordinary power that he exercised. Then, however, it was precisely in these big, pacesetting enterprises that even this institutional tie was broken by subsequent developments. The decision-making power passed over to management personnel, and "absentee ownership"[19] meant that the owners themselves did nothing more than draw their dividends.[20] There emerged the well-known "managerial regime,"[21] which today sets the pattern. The enterprise secured its independence in relation to the capital on which it was run, and turned "into an autonomous body after the fashion of a philanthropic foundation, or, rather, after the fashion of a state."[22] But having achieved independence of the institution, it was now carried on by a person at the summit, who himself had hardly any institutional support from outside. In other words, personal responsibility

[19] Thorstein Veblen, *Absentee Ownership and Business Enterprise in Recent Times; The Case of America* (New York: Augustus M. Kelley, 1964).
[20] Helmut Schelsky, "Industrie- und Betriebssoziologie," *Soziologie,* ed. Arnold Gehlen and Helmut Schelsky (Düsseldorf, 1955), p. 165.
[21] James Burnham, *The Managerial Revolution* (Bloomington, Ind.: Indiana University Press, 1960).
[22] Walter Rathenau, cited by Schelsky, *loc. cit.*

at the summit still carried on the enterprise exclusively, even more so than before.

At the same time, however, the nature of this responsibility at the summit changed; it became, if we may say so, more personal than ever. Among the qualities that someone in management must possess today, the "ability to manage men" is always included. What that involves can be seen from the preceding pages. First, it is the art of leaving the employee the necessary scope for personal responsibility; secondly, it is the capacity to bring about and cultivate self-reliant cooperation between subordinates of equal rank, and to interfere with it as little as possible; and thirdly, the ability to work in mutual confidence with subordinates who are chosen by their colleagues to represent them, and who are therefore no longer mere subordinates but negotiators with equal rights. If we add the remark that the manager, in contrast to the earlier entrepreneur, is today generally not a lonely figure at the summit, but a member of a directing body with which he must collaborate in reaching decisions, the new nature of the personal existence embodied here becomes evident: to the individualization, which goes on as before, there is now added the crucial question of one's relationship to one's counterpart, a person who stands on his own feet and who, like his superior, also bears responsibility. The individual who stands vis-à-vis another, however, is more a person than was the solitary individual who was able to demand unconditional obedience.

This kind of responsibility is not confined to the summit. It is also applicable to all the intermediate authorities who bear responsibility, for they too have to work together with other people. Today, in fact, the widening sphere of cooperation and responsibility demands this personal kind of exercise of responsibility, in greater or lesser degree, from everyone in the business. So we can say of the modern class of "managers" what has been true of every class of leaders in history: their particular qualities can and must impress themselves on their subordinates. The course that modern business is taking demands a similar personal responsibility at all levels.

7

The State in a World

of Organizations

The state has played a dual role in the development of the organization. On the one hand, following the precedent set by the church, it has done a great deal to develop the new principle further and then to secure wide acceptance for it in secular life. With its organizational structures of bureaus and agencies, the standing army, legislature, and cabinet, it became a model for the organizational categories "business" and "association." In its systematic legislation it appropriated the principle of flexibility. By deliberately limiting its own powers as a state based on law, it incorporated into its structure the principle of limited aims. And, finally, with its division of powers and its commitment to the inviolability of the private sphere, it became the champion of personal freedom, which is an absolutely essential characteristic of any advanced organization. In all of this, the state was a powerful means of developing and disseminating the new principle of organization.

On the other hand, however, in the seventeenth and eighteenth centuries the state drew to itself the whole social regalia of the old traditional institutions with their halo of sacrosanctity, thus creating breathing space for secularized social bodies, but itself retaining the odor of sanctity longer than any other body. In the "grace of God" mottoes of kings and princes, in the alliance of "throne and altar," in the battle cry "For God, king, and country," and lastly in the belief in a "sacred fatherland," the sacrosanct devotion which was general in the medieval "Holy Empire" has lasted longest; it persists even today. Present-day Germans, after the recent flagrant abuses of a sacrosanct "fatherland" concept, are now left with little more than a secularized attitude of disenchantment toward their state, the more so as the Federal Republic must be regarded, constitutionally, as a makeshift affair, and not, in its present partial form, as a "fatherland." In the present situation, and probably for a long time to come, the expression "sacred fatherland" will have a hollow ring. With all this, the state shows all the characteristics of an "organization." But it would be preposterous to regard it as "merely" an organization, and so put it on the same level as a baseball club or a margarine factory. One expects a state, even a makeshift one, to be able to claim more devotion than a "purely rational" organization could.

It is apparent that some conceptual clarity is needed here. If it is to exist at all, a state undoubtedly must demand more than a purely rational relationship of its citizens to its own existence; it cannot remain viable if their interest in it is simply selfish. But this attribute is one that the state has in common with all organizations. We have already noticed repeatedly in looking at the association and the business that, to endure, an organization needs that "something extra" in the way of commitment, and that this is not to be had from a purely rational relationship.

It is therefore incorrect to distinguish between the state as an entity with more than "purely rational" ties, and organizations with "purely rational" ties, for there are no viable organizations whatever that exist for purely rational considerations. Of course, within this circle of basically related entities there are gradations in the scope and ranking of responsibilities. And it is here that the state must claim a special position, for its responsibility is more comprehensive than that of any association or business. It is the bearer and guarantor of the rule of law, which supports all the other organizations. And it remains the only organization that can legitimately use force. These and other of its enduring attributes give the state, as an institution, a dignity that towers far above that of the other organizations. For this reason the state becomes, in a profound sense, a *Schicksalsgemeinschaft* — a community bound together unto life and death. Therefore it cannot disavow certain traditional cohesive forces which emanated from it in its past days as an institution, and by which it lived: loyalty, integrity in its civil servants, respect for the official organs of the state. These are forces within the state that enable it to function, even if — and even as — it is understood to be an "organization."

Authority and Freedom

We encounter the same situation from a different angle if we ask whether, and how far, we are still to regard the power of the state today as "authority." In constitutional law and sociology, this concept is still widely employed, not only with respect to the power of the state, but also with reference to power structures in general.

The question whether or not we continue to apply the concept of "authority" to the structures of modern society might be viewed as a mere quibbling over words. What is at issue, however, is a very important question that lies behind the words: What are the bases of governmental rule today? Or, alternatively: Do we not find that a significant change in these bases has been in process for quite some time?

Arnold Gehlen has recently expressed some misgivings on this score, speaking of the "increasing unsuitability of the concept 'authority' " when applied to life in the modern state. After all, he argues, authority signifies "some sort of existential acceptance of duty by man." Governmental rule today, however, is exercised more as "a strictly limited power to regulate, a power which is made inevitable — and legitimate — by the obvious constraint inherent in the very facts of the situation and which is strictly limited to the sphere of the particular regulated undertaking."[1]

This assertion of a purely objectivized governmental system, devoid of existential acceptance of obligation on the part of the citizens, is clearly exaggerated. To mention only one point, it ignores the right, and need, of the state to demand that a civil servant take an oath before he assumes office, or that a citizen take an oath in court. An oath is a distinctive mark of a sacrosanct institution; it binds the whole person. To that extent the institution that is the "state" has undoubtedly remained an "authority."

Nevertheless, Gehlen's statement points in an illuminating way to an important change of emphasis in the relationship of the state to its citizens. In Germany, for example, the constitution of the Federal Republic indicates that the main stress of the tie between citizen and state lies not in the authoritarian-institutional but in the personal sphere. It is striking that the constitution knows no "constitutional duties," but only "constitutional rights," which indeed guarantee existential freedom within a very broad framework. These rights are laid down, not simply as rights, but as "basic" rights, and they are explicitly made irrevocable. That means that the whole of the statutory law of the state is to be erected on the foundation of this existential freedom. In this connection we may again recall Mitteis' description of law as "the weapon of the individual."[2] In the constitution, even the acceptance of the ultimate duty, hitherto regarded as not open to question — the offering of one's life in the armed services — is not demanded when it is forbidden by the personal authority of one's conscience (Art. 4, par. 3 GG). Here we have direct evidence of where the really overriding authority is seen to reside. It is in line with

[1] Arnold Gehlen, "Industriegesellschaft und Staat (Über einige Triebkräfte des politischen Lebens der Gegenwart)," *Wort und Wahrheit,* IX, No. 11 (Sept., 1956), 670.
[2] See Heinrich Mitteis, "Das Recht als Waffe des Individuums," *Die Rechtsidee in der Geschichte* (Weimar, 1957), pp. 514 ff.

this, too, that service in the armed forces is regarded less as a duty to the "fatherland" than as a duty to defend freedom — that personal freedom guaranteed by the constitution.

If that is the position of the citizen within the framework of the state, then the state must govern accordingly. Here, in view of the fact that the citizen is regarded more in terms of the rights to which he is entitled than of the duties to which he is subject, primary emphasis must be on doing justice to the "constraint inherent in the very facts of the situation." In keeping with the nature of the organization, this must be done with "limited power" — limited, that is, to what the facts dictate. Limitation of jurisdiction by division of powers was extolled long ago by its great advocate, Montesquieu, as a guarantee of freedom. Indeed both institutional limitation and the personal freedom which it conditions and which is in turn conditioned by it — both belong to the principle of the "organization."

Nevertheless, again and again one sees that the principle of the organization inevitably includes also an inexhaustible "extra" of commitment, and that the "constraint inherent in the facts" cannot be purely rational. So, too, in the state. The modern politician, elected for a limited term of office and constitutionally dependent on the "confidence" of the voters, cannot regard his ties with his constituency in a purely rational way. But an "existential acceptance of duty" is greatly devalued by "constitutional rights." The stress, therefore, lies on a bond that is the opposite of authoritarian obligation. The latter was an existential commitment laid on the subject by the ruler; today, however, everything tends toward responsibility in the form of a self-imposed obligation in a relationship of confidence. And this relationship involves a citizen who has likewise been given, in his constitutional rights, the responsibility of self-imposed obligation. But this kind of relationship is nothing other than personal responsibility. We may therefore say that authority is a form of institutional commitment, and that governance on the organizational pattern combines that commitment with personal responsibility. And history is moving from the one to the other. We can repeatedly see a shifting of the stress from a basis in institutional regulations to the new personal basis.

Yet it may be asked, not unreasonably, whether, in the historical realm, corporate life on a purely personal basis is at all possible. In any case, although that basis is a sound one, the structures that are raised on it are very much less stable and more precarious than were those of the traditional institutional kind. The states in the world of the seventeenth and eighteenth centuries represented a transitional mixture of both types, a very purposefully constructed state machinery being built up on the authentic "authority" principle of the "grace of God." And in all the monarchies of our own time, the old "existential-acceptance-of-duty" kind of authority is still kept at the top, in the shape of the crown, although logically it contradicts a constitution based on fundamental rights. These states have remained remarkably stable in spite of the logical contradiction, for illogical relationships that have been allowed to grow have always lasted better than those that have been constructed throughout on logical principles. But even in those states that have retained no institutional "authority" structures, old authoritarian characteristics still exercise their influence as "cohesive forces" in the edifice of the state.

To repeat: The existential acceptance of duty in the "fatherland" concept, in the ethos of the civil service, in the military way of thinking, in respect for the organs of state — this and much more besides are relics of the days when the state was wholly or predominantly an instrument of "authority." It is difficult for us to relinquish these "cohesive forces," but we must remember that they are capital amassed in bygone times, which wastes away. Capital that the present time can amass has a different look.

Personalization as a Consequence of Democracy

The shifting of the basis of the state from institutional to personal responsibility has other causes as well, or, shall we say, can be demonstrated from other points of view. Personalization is also — remarkable as it may seem — the consequence of a phenomenon which one might at first suppose would work the other way: it is the result of the development toward universal suffrage, that is, toward mass democracy.

What happened here was, in principle, exactly the same as what happened in the development of associations and federations. In the older city republics, as in the beginnings of self-government and constitutional rule in the eighteenth and nineteenth centuries, the tasks confronting national and communal governing bodies were quite straightforward and could be easily surveyed and mastered. Public life then did not yet possess the infinite variety it has today, and so, generally speaking, the skills that were provided by the circle of responsible people from its own world of aristocracy, commerce, and handicraft, were adequate. This circle was not large, and its members were known to each other, whether in the republic of Venice, the Hanseatic town of Hamburg, the thirteen North American colonies at the time they declared their independence, or in the self-governing Prussian towns of Freiherr von Stein. Thus the community was in fact governed by this circle of "citizens," and there was no reason in principle why any public office could not be occupied by anyone from that group — allowing, of course, for individual differences within it. There was genuine public scrutiny in such a case, where every enfranchised citizen was adequately informed to pass a balanced judgment on matters of common concern. Each new generation was carefully initiated into the well-tested results of past experience, into the existing conditions and the established ways of handling them. As long as that state of affairs lasted, the old community life rested solidly on firm ground.

Today it is a quite different story. In the state, as in local self-government, the number of voters has risen enormously, running into many millions in the great democracies. Even within the framework of a local community in a big city, the people concerned cannot all know each other. At the same time the size and scope of the problems have also increased enormously, and to cope with them requires special skills which few possess. Genuine public scrutiny combined with good all-round knowledge and balanced judgment is now out of the question.

These changes in the preconditions of political cooperation have hardly, even yet, sunk into our minds. As a result, the widespread lack of interest in political questions, an inevitable consequence of the changed preconditions, is still being combatted with fruitless appeals that feed on the old conceptions of a system of government run by amateurs.

Actually, political life has in the meantime necessarily taken on a quite different character, which has already proved workable, but of which we have not yet become fully conscious. As in the case of associations and federations, the initiative has long since passed from the membership as a whole to a small circle of people who carry on the public's affairs, either without pay or as their full-time work. Here, as in the federations, men and women are needed who through inclination, educational background, and experience possess the necessary qualifications or who can acquire them in adequate measure during the course of their employment.

The comparison with the federations does not rest here merely on an outward similarity in their historical development. On the contrary, the most practical way to get into national and local politics is through responsible involvement in parties or federations like the pressure groups.

Today our public life already rests more on the businesslike and responsible work of these individuals than on widespread political interest among the voters. Election propaganda has found this out and takes full account of it. It does not now appeal, as it still did in the twenties, to political "idealism," to a particular attitude toward the state, or to a longing for a particular system of government in the future. Instead, there is a striking unanimity among all parties in displaying "faces." At election time a cluster of handbills and billboards look like portrait galleries, and handbills have largely shed the character of the "poster."

As to the effectiveness of these "faces" the decisive factor is not only whether the persons displayed have knowledge and ability, but also whether they radiate a certain indefinable "extra" that wins the voters' confidence. Until the thirties, elections were votes expressing conviction in certain ideas; today they are expressions of confidence in persons. And these individuals not only possess certain specific qualities; they are also "persons," which here means they possess the ability to create and foster a relationship of confidence.

But in this transition from the old kind of constitution, which counted on the voluntary service of a small group of "citizens," to modern democracy, we can see another feature of what "person" means today. Where public life was formerly carried on by a comparatively small circle of people entitled to vote and exercise responsibility, that circle always bore the very deep imprint of the institution. The "eligible" families of the old city republics represented a homogeneous group of families, boasting long pedigrees and admitting replenishments from the outside only rarely and cautiously. Even into the nineteenth century, English self-government in the plains was a matter for the nobility. And the broader-based city government of Freiherr von Stein was manned solely by heads of families drawn from various levels of society but shaped by that stratified society; even though his reform breached the barriers of class and rank, these distinctions were slow to disintegrate, and did not disappear until much later. It is true that the people who created and put into use the constitution of the United States were emigrants or sons of emigrants who had of set purpose turned their backs on the European class system, but they themselves in their colonists' federations and church communities again established a communal life that exerted profound influence, one that persists to the present day.

Where an elected representative who came from such circles entered on a public office, therefore, his personal qualities lay primarily in the general characteristics that united him with his constituents. That is what gave these "personalities" their firm and resolute nature and, consequently, a sure basis for openness to the political realities. We must always understand the "personality" of the late eighteenth and early nineteenth centuries in relation to this fluid, transitional situation, in which the old institutional mentality was still influential. The old orders inherited from the stratified society still provided the individual with cohesion and structures, but at the same time he was obliged, as an "individual," to keep his mind open to new situations and new requirements. In previous times the class mentality usually meant that a certain limitation of outlook was predominant, which was surmounted only by a really great pioneering statesman and a man of exceptional creative ability.

Today when individuals are prominent in public life, inspire confidence, and make good as persons, we nearly always find that they still possess the characteristics of earlier types. The scholar, the military man, the craftsman, the farmer, can still be seen in elected representatives. Indeed it is these very characteristics which give them stability, firmness, and direction. But what could be achieved in former centuries only by the really great, what even the personalities of the late eighteenth and early nineteenth centuries combined only very cautiously with their traditional background, is demanded of present-day political figures as their main virtue — complete openness to new realities. To achieve anything of real value today presupposes an unprejudiced willingness to grapple with everything, and to exclude nothing offhand. In this respect, too, the basis of our public life has shifted from the institutional to the personal, and the balance has gone down on the personal side. Thus we see another element that must be included in the concept of the "personal."

8

Social Pluralism and the

Problem of Integration

When we speak of the pluralism of our social world, we generally have in mind the obvious fact that modern social and political life consists of a multiplicity of organizations, interest groups, and pressure groups that form no integral unity. There are all kinds of ties linking them with one another, but at the same time they are separated by profound antitheses. Our everyday experience tells us what a danger this is: individual interest constantly threatens to swamp the common interest, and rifts threaten to become gaping chasms separating things that belong together. The danger is all the greater when such a society is threatened by some unusual state of emergency, by political and economic crises. How can it withstand such strains?

The unity that is threatened by this pluralism, however, is not simply that of the society but also that of the life of people within it. According to the principle of organization, everyone is today involved with his varied interests and connections, in many places simultaneously, and his life is filled with all these organizational ties; and so the rifts that split the society run not merely through groups of people, but even through the existence of the individual himself. In contrast to the more integral institutions of the old stratified society, modern organizations do not make a person a unity, but bring their own antitheses and diversities not only *to* him, but squarely *into* him. In a great many cases this causes serious inner conflicts. Consider, for instance, the strain imposed when one's vocational and family obligations pull in opposite directions; or the clash of loyalties to which a shop steward is exposed as a member of the company staff as well as of the union; or the extremely varied human demands that have to be satisfied by a worker who also serves on the town council. The pluralism of society is a problem, not only for society, but also for the life of the individual.

The question arises, therefore, whether there is no integrating force that will unite and consolidate all these different elements. From what source, what set of conceptions, what responsibility can the forces that now diverge, clash, and conflict be coordinated, harmonized, and held together? This is basically the question of political power in its pure and original sense. And it is a further crucial question for the organization: Does the organization itself possess the strength and the ability to harmonize and integrate its own world? Can it coordinate only at times and in part, but not entirely?

The Political and the Libertarian Solutions

In his critical analysis *Landmarks of Tomorrow,* Peter Drucker gives a concise and startling answer to this question: "We are without an effective institution of political integration and order."[1] This sentence, which comes at the beginning of a chapter on the present-day state, asserts that the state at one time accomplished the task of integration but is no longer able to do so effectively, that is, adequately.

The classical definition of social integration by the state was given by Hegel in his *Philosophy of Right.*[2] Hegel makes a

[1] Peter Drucker, *Landmarks of Tomorrow* (New York: Harper & Row, 1959), p. 195.
[2] Georg Wilhelm Friedrich Hegel, *Philosophy of Right,* ed. and trans. T. M. Knox (London: Oxford University Press, 1942).

fundamental distinction (par. 157) between "civil society" and the "constitution of the state." Civil society has no unity; it is in a "state of discord" ("*Zustand der Entzweiung*") and of "the relative" ("*Standpunkt des Relativen*"). Its members are joined together "as self-subsistent individuals,"[3] and this union is established in a formal and external way through "needs" and through the outward security provided by the "legal constitution." This conception was first put forward in 1821, while the dissolution of the old stratified society by the Prussian reforms was still in progress, and associations and industries were still in their earliest, rudimentary beginnings. Nevertheless the emerging new social principle of "organization" was grasped and characterized with great insight and precision by Hegel. He said that what constituted the functional and cohesive basis of this "relative" and "discordant" world was that which in his time was still intact as the true social reality: the state constitution as "the end and actuality of both the substantial universal order and the public life devoted thereto."[4] Through this constitution civil society is "brought back to and welded into unity . . . ."[5] It is worthwhile to pause for a moment over these statements. For we see here, as if brought to an intense focus by a magnifying glass, much of what we have been discussing in these pages; at the same time it becomes clear that the question about the foundations of society is simultaneously the question about its integration. In the old days, social life was determined by the institution; essential reality rested in the institution, not in the individual. Then the rising modern state undermined the whole kaleidoscopic medieval world of the institution. It took over the substance of the feudal ties and brotherhoods, which were henceforth to exist only on the authority of the state and with its consent, and which were finally to disappear. In Hegel's time this process was already complete with respect to the emancipation of the serfs, the granting of freedom to run a business or

[3] *Ibid.*, p. 110.
[4] *Ibid.*
[5] *Ibid.*

pursue an occupation of one's choosing, and other reforms. Thus Hegel could claim that the state was the true "end and actuality of . . . the substantial universal order" and the basis and setting of all other "relative" entities.

The state, though still a sacrosanct traditional institution and at the same time already an organization, assimilated the other sacrosanct traditional institutions and paved the way for the rise of the world of organizations, a development Hegel perceived with clarity. Since organizations themselves, as Hegel likewise remarks, possess no sustaining power, no "substantiality," and no unity, they have to derive these from another sector. In his own time Hegel saw organizations as newly weaned from the maternal breast that had protected and nourished them: the state. The state had that "substantial reality"; it was, as Hegel says in another passage, "an end sufficient in itself," something "reasonable in and for itself."

Hegel's stretching and straining of the concept of the state was already an indication that its unique position was beginning to be undermined. The state has at no time achieved such an exclusive and comprehensive integration of the entire social body as Hegel ascribed to it, not even in the days when it had everything in its tutelage. But in the century that has elapsed since his time, many new kinds of forces and developments have further restricted and undermined the possibility that the state might constitute the integrating, all-embracing horizon of a complete structure of society.

In domestic affairs the state has devoted itself to the safeguarding of fundamental rights, renouncing to a great extent its right of veto and control; the legal code it has established constitutes a very loose framework within which many conflicting situations are possible. As to foreign affairs, political developments after the Second World War have often compelled the hitherto jealously guarded national sovereignty of the state to give way to greater integration; in addition, complex economic and social networks cut across state boundaries. Further, the social boundaries that Hegel was still able to set so precisely have become so fluid that often they are scarcely discernible. With secularization the character of the state has moved a good deal closer to that of the social organizations, and the state itself, as entrepreneur and as welfare and insurance agency, has entered upon numerous activities that compete with private organizations. As a result it has not only diminished its own power to draw these organizations together into a unity, but it has itself become pluralistic, and the question of integration has already emerged within its own apparatus of bureaus, institutions, public enterprises, and insurance schemes.

On the other hand, of course, the state today still exercises an important integrating function. We need only think of the system of law that forms an indispensable basis of the whole world of organizations. We may recollect that that system is developing more and more into one of "social right"[6] that aims at averting the worst consequences of our great social inequalities, thus bridging or at least narrowing the rifts in society. Closely connected with this is government social policy, by which the state not only tries to assume responsibility for the worst cases of distress that are not otherwise provided for, but also acts as a redistributor of income on a large scale through old-age pensions, public assistance payments, retirement pensions paid for by taxation or compulsory contributions. And of course it exercises a strong supervisory, and therefore integrating, influence on the life of society through its monetary and economic policy, its assistance to education, its stimulation of building activity, and so on. Even in our time, therefore, the state is an integrating force; and a quite modern theory of the state, such as Rudolf Smend's theory of integration, tries to find here the real criterion of the state. To that extent, no doubt, Peter Drucker's remark is exaggerated. But, like Gehlen's exaggerated judgment, referred to above, about the inappropriateness of the concept of authority, Drucker's remark has the merit of pointing out that the character of the state has turned sharply in a new direction.

Now, the criticism of the state's claim to a comprehensive

[6] See p. 101, n. 2 above.

integrating function is not new. It was given articulate expression, with significant historical effects, by the libertarian movement of the nineteenth century. As Johannes Messner puts it, the social theory of classical libertarianism asserted that "the best social order results from the freedom of the individual, unfettered as far as possible by social restrictions; the less the freedom of the individual in the pursuit of his own interests is restricted by checks imposed by society, and the more society itself ensures individual freedom, the better and the more surely will the welfare of the individual, as well as that of society, be achieved."[7]

That was the line of argument against the paternal system of state tutelage and in favor of giving free play to individual initiative. This produced great results in the old industrial countries. It released forces which successfully developed and implanted the new social models and the new patterns of production. The triumph of these forces is also evident in the modern governmental structures of the Western countries, which in their constitutions have expressly guaranteed "individual freedom."

The libertarian belief that the general pursuit of individual self-interest would as a matter of course lead to integration is not quite so mistaken as is often supposed today in the wake of political and economic disasters. That becomes evident when we think what "interest" and the "pursuit of interest" really mean in the modern social context. We generally add to "interest," either implicitly or explicitly, the word "self(ish)," and in the pursuit of "self-interest" we see a force that disintegrates society and must therefore be kept within bounds by socially beneficent forces working in the opposite direction. But that is a very one-sided view.

There is no doubt that interests are in the first place "individual interests," and that in principle they come up against opposing interests, so that there is a perpetual clash. Generally these have been market interests, since the widespread com-

[7] Johannes Messner, "Liberalismus," *Staatslexikon,* ed. H. Sacher, Vol. III (Freiburg im Breisgau, 1929), col. 973.

mercialization of life in the nineteenth century. Either one wants to sell goods or services for the highest price possible, or to sell more of them than the competitor, or one is trying to buy them for the lowest price possible. In addition, there are demands on the state for subsidies and other payments, and there are anxieties about high taxes, efforts to get preferential treatment through new laws, and so on.

These interests nearly always have one peculiarity: they are multilayered, and the interest of one stratum is at variance with that of the others. In market transactions, for instance, there is a clash of interest between buyer and seller, the former wanting low prices and the latter wanting high prices. At the same time, however, they both have a parallel interest, namely, that the transaction should indeed take place. That is a force that generally compels the originally divergent interests to come together and that fixes the actual price as a compromise produced by the parallelogram of forces. The two opposing interests are overlaid by a third, the public interest, which is, shall we say, that the existing monetary system should not be shaken by an excessively high price level. This public interest exerts but little perceptible pressure at the time when the transaction is consummated. The consequences of ignoring it do not become apparent till later, when it is too late; but they do appear, and the perceptive person will take this public interest into account as being indirectly his own interest too, when properly understood.

Two more examples may be cited. In a federation representing similar interests, firms of a certain economic group are joined together — let us say, automobile manufacturers and distributors, or makers of machine tools. The members of the federation have numerous common interests in relation to the state or the industry as such. But at the same time they are competitors in the market, who want to entice away from each other as many customers as they can.

There is a similar clash of interest in the relationship between the management of a company and its employees. The one side has to "buy" its labor on the most favorable terms possible, since wages are a factor in costs and may impede a firm's ability to compete. The other side has to "sell" its labor for the highest price it can get, since a worker's wages are the basis of his whole family's existence. But at the same time, both sides have a pressing common interest in selling as much as they can of their joint product on the most favorable terms possible.

On closer examination, therefore, we find almost everywhere that "interests" force people apart in one respect, but that they also contain an element that draws people together. These two elements are often in stiff opposition to each other. As a rule, this opposition can be neither eliminated nor harmonized, and there remains only the possibility of compromise from one case to another, or the deliberate decision in favor of one side at the expense of the other. And always standing mutely by is the public interest, which, properly understood, is indirectly a self-interest and which is always ready to avenge itself remorselessly if it is grossly and repeatedly injured.

So the play of interests is not just a confused medley of individual forces, but something that also contains a positive tendency toward unity, though that unity is one of tension and can never be permanently and solidly established. It embodies a constant challenge to the interested parties, one that arises out of the facts of the particular situation.

On the other hand, however, the self-regulating power operative in the functioning of the social system, with everyone simply pursuing his own interest, has proved to be inadequate. Through labor laws and social legislation, by limiting the concept of property, and in much else, society has had to reintroduce barriers and restrictions, so that, theory notwithstanding, the welfare of the individual and of society may be achieved better and more surely.

But no final solution of the problem can be expected from the erection of these barriers and restrictions. For the responsibility for unity is now thrown back onto the state, and it has been made clear that, while the state certainly has permanent obligations in this direction, its possibilities of achieving social integration have likewise starkly diminished. Indeed, this persistent pushing of responsibility back onto the state ever since the end of the nineteenth century has immensely increased the burden of the state's responsibilities. This has meant the further pluralization of the state itself, thus making it more and more difficult for the state to fulfil its task of social integration. The state itself was caught up in the mesh of diverse and competing forces, and its machinery, like its legislation, lost that transparency of the whole which is the precondition of all integration. Thus the growth of the state's responsibilities actually reduced its means of coping with them.

Integration Through Personal Responsibility

The way out of this dilemma seems to lie in the realization that both the appeal to the state and the libertarian faith in automatic regulation stem from the same antiquated world of concepts, and that today that world of concepts is valid only within limits. Something new has appeared alongside it, and is steadily gaining in importance. The "old" way is responsibility based on an order or institution, and the "new" is responsibility borne by the person.

The responsible order: that was the state, or, more accurately, the "constitution of the state," in Hegel's words. The cohesive power of the state, says Hegel, is solely "the fundamental sense of order which everybody possesses."[8] The whole of the Middle Ages had based its thinking on a great all-embracing *ordo,* a comprehensive ordering of things; and the modern state, as the heir of medieval institutions, had concentrated this way of thinking on itself.

Libertarianism retained the *ordo* mentality, although it expressly assigned "limits to the state's functions," as Von Humboldt said.[9] People thought they could confine the state's laws to a minimum, because there were also supposed to be reliable "natural laws" in the social order. In any case, confidence in

[8] Hegel, *op. cit.,* par. 268, p. 282.
[9] See p. 57 above.

the automatic adjustment of the play of social forces rests primarily on a deistic religious faith in a world order that provided for, and effected, a "prestabilized harmony" — a unity — for the life of man in community, if only that order were allowed free play. Again, this was a kind of survival of the medieval *ordo* mentality, and the hostile brothers — "conservative thinking" (for state action) and "liberal thinking" (for freedom of action) — proved to be children of the same mother. For libertarianism, which demanded the freedom of the individual, saw the fountainhead of order, not in the individual himself, but in a harmony that was effected over the heads of individuals. In both cases there was a belief in a concept of order, the difference being that in one case the divine world order worked directly, and in the other it worked through the mediation of earthly authorities commissioned by God. In fact, both conservative and liberal thought discerned the rise of pluralism and affirmed it, and also saw the need for it to be integrated, but neither found *in* it the force that could bring about such unity. Instead, both of them put their trust in a power from outside, a closed, encircling horizon that was to bind this multiplicity into a whole.

Both of these conceptions survive today, and continue to have an influence on our corporate life. But they have already reached their limits. Today we cannot entrust either to the state or to a mechanism of automatic regulation the whole responsibility for holding our social fabric together, or for ensuring that the rifts which run squarely through the individual do not lead to intolerable stresses and conflicts. But where is the place where this responsibility can effectively be borne, or, shall we say (since we should be asking, not about possibilities, but about facts), where is this responsibility already being shouldered at this moment?

The answer must be: the new locus of responsibility lies at the very heart of the pluralism of society, where people have not yet ventured to look for it, because they have seen at work there nothing but what is relative, selfish, and disruptive — it lies with the person. The responsibility that is borne by the person is indeed a personal one, and not one that lives on *ordo* concepts. It is once more the same thing that we have seen again and again from a variety of angles: the place of responsibility is shifting, and with it the nature of responsibility is also changing. What does that mean in this case?

In his *Theorie des gegenwärtigen Zeitalters*[10] Hans Freyer has contrasted the different principles on which the social constitutions of the old style and of the modern world of organizations are constructed. He describes the earlier world as having been built on the pattern of the *oikos* (household), whereas the integrating principle of the modern world is that of "circulation."

An *oikos*, a "whole house," was a largely self-sufficient (autarchic) cosmos. Larger federations were composed of houses of the same or similar composition, and there was little division of labor. Until the early nineteenth century the state, too, regarded itself as a great housekeeping (i.e., "economic") concern set over a particular geographical territory, the "father of the people" being at its head. The idea of this old paternalistic world survives even today in the word "economy" (from *oikonomia,* "management of a household"). Local self-sufficiency (autarchy), of which the normative and predominant type was the farm, meant that economic malfunctionings were generally confined to a small area and rarely extended beyond that area to other spheres. The world of organizations, however, has departed in principle from the axiom of self-sufficiency for a single entity. Where each entity confines itself to a limited circle of responsibilities, as an organization does, each entity is necessarily involved with all other entities. Each is dependent on all of the others, through an intricate network of connecting ties, and when malfunctionings and crises occur, they reverberate through the whole network and back to their point of origin. We need only think of the general interdependence that has emerged from the general adoption of a money economy and the resulting currency problems. And this is only one example of many kinds of interdependence.

[10] Hans Freyer, *Theorie des gegenwärtigen Zeitalters* (Stuttgart: Deutsche Verlags-Anstalt, 1955).

Not only has this interdependence at times involved every sector of a nation, but the economic and other repercussions have spread almost at once beyond the national boundaries. The consequence is that political responsibility is diffused in all directions, whether people realize it and take it into account or not. Decisions affecting the whole society are made not only by government officials, but by every organization that makes decisions anywhere in the immense total network. Everyone, in Freyer's slightly macabre expression, "can have his hand on the throat of the whole society." But that means that the whole social structure has become political, and that the state's political monopoly is permanently broken. In this respect, too, the boundaries between state and society have become fluid. Together the two form a single great network through which the succession of actions and reactions is constantly circulating.

This network has emerged because organizations as such have the special characteristic of being, in principle, open entities, whose life and mode of operation necessarily consist in a complex system of relationships with many other organizations. They may be regarded as in some degree points of intersection in a network of relationships.

Think, for instance, of all the people with whom the management of a manufacturing business has to be in touch. There are the suppliers of raw materials, machines, tools, and fuel. There are the customers. There is government in the form of the internal revenue service, the department of commerce, the local officials, and so forth. There are chambers of commerce and employers' and trade associations. There are labor unions, insurance companies, tax experts, auditors, the press. Anyone acquainted with the world of business could easily add to the list. Similarly with federations. A federation representing a certain sector of business has to deal with the industry, the wholesale trade, the retail trade, the labor unions, government officials, consumers' unions, vocational schools, the press, the chamber of commerce, and so on.

In this sense, therefore, the great network is connected with and through each of its nodal points. Every form, every federation, every department and agency of government is such a nodal point. It is intrinsic to the nature of an organization that it constitutes a node in a great network. Of course, some organizations have a wide radius of action and a great deal of influence on the whole, while others have only a narrow radius. The former incur a greater responsibility for the integration of the whole than do the latter. Each of them, however, bears some responsibility for the whole, and bears it inseparably from its responsibility for itself.

To carry our argument through to its conclusion, we should recall what crucial power and responsibility the organization of today bears and exercises. This responsibility is of the personal kind. The organization, then, has a decisive role to play today in the task of integrating the very diverse whole.

That corresponds exactly to the facts of the case. For in its relation to the outside world the organization, insofar as it is an institution, is tied to rigidity, fixity, and separateness. The kind of responsibility we have been discussing, however, is one of openness to the outside world, of flexibility, of constantly finding appropriate responses to ever-new situations, possibilities, difficulties, and conflicts. What is called for is a continual building of temporary bridges in all directions, as well as imagination and a wealth of ideas. All these, however, are personal qualities; they are not proper to an institution as institution.

But it is not only as a responsible member of organizations that the person achieves this integration. His own personal life, too, is a "nodal-point existence."[11] That, in fact, is why the clashes and antagonisms of society run squarely through his personal life; that is why the person is in danger of being rent by a social world that has not been brought to unity. And so there is no choice: the individual cannot wait for a neutral force to smooth out and reconcile the antagonisms between his family and his occupation, between federation and government, employer and employee, buyer and seller, till a restored world encircles him and comes to his rescue. On the contrary, he has to face the antagonisms himself whenever he is drawn

[11] Arnold Gehlen, *Die Seele im technischen Zeitalter. Sozialpsychologische Probleme in der industriellen Gesellschaft* (Hamburg, 1957), p. 109.

into them; he must stick to his position, and do the right thing from one case to another — either have his way, or give way, or find the right sort of compromise, always rendering the other person his due appreciation, or striking the right balance between two duties that struggle within himself. Every one of us is, in some way or other, subjected to this kind of tension. But anyone who deals with these antagonisms in a personal kind of responsibility, whether as politician or government official, corporation executive or businessman, physician or tax expert, deals with them vicariously for other people too, relieving the latter at least to some extent of the tensions and antagonisms of our social world.

Finally, we would call to mind once more Peter Drucker's words: "We are without an effective institution of political integration and order."[12] Fortunately that is an overstatement. The state still does a great deal, even in the Hegelian sense, toward integrating "relative" and "discordant" forces. But here, too, we are living on diminishing capital that is not being replenished. Even in the state itself, the course of development is firmly in the direction of the new, personal basis, and of integration through personal responsibility.

Nor was the approach of libertarianism a wrong one. A great deal in modern society really is self-regulating, just because the force within the interests themselves is not only divisive but also cohesive. But each time divisive and cohesive factors have to be weighed in the balance, there is needed a responsibility that cannot be achieved by the individual as an individual, as a social atom. The individual, however, is in fact not a social atom. His existence consists in many relationships, which are here to be understood under the rubric "person." These final considerations have added an important feature to our portrait of the person: it is his responsibility to produce a tension-filled unity out of the variety of conflicting forces.

[12] Drucker, *op. cit.*, p. 195.

Part III

The Person

9

Personal Life in the Age

of the Organization

Organization and Person

Our discussion of the possible integration of the pluralistic society may well conclude our survey of the world of organizations. In the present context, this survey had to be brief, and it has been possible to stress only a few factors in the immense array of facts and relationships. But in order to make possible some kind of meaningful progress through this array without wasting time on nonessentials, we asked two questions at the outset: First, what forces give stability to the flexible and changeable modern world, after the old stabilizing sacrosanct traditional orders have been eliminated except for a few surviving traces? Secondly, how is one to assess the "individualization" of man in society, a fact which has undoubtedly been evident for a long time, at least since the Renaissance and the Reformation, and which, among other things, has been given general recognition in modern law? Very different answers have been given to these questions in the preceding chapters, and it is time to summarize them and put them in order.

The answers can, in the first place, be reduced to a common denominator insofar as the phenomena we have been consid-

144

ering all fall within the sphere of "organizations." Everything
that has been said here, therefore, contributes to a more precise
knowledge of the organization generally. The organization is
the dominating principle of our modern public institutions. The
three basic types in which the organization appears in concrete
form — association, business, and state — are in their nature
different developments of the same principle. Our discussion
brought to light the surprising fact that these three types, as
they proceeded in their development and came to be securely
established, began to resemble one another closely. For that
reason, what we have observed with regard to the three types
can now be summarized quite readily as statements about the
organization as such.

With regard to the first question, then, we saw that the
organization lives on the basis of the two centers of responsible
human guidance: the institution and the person. An institution
it certainly is. It has public scrutiny and reciprocal surveillance.
It operates with some form of adjudication and disciplinary
authority. Its membership is marked off from those outside. It
is based on a constitution and a balance of services rendered.
It is designed for stability and permanence. All this is obvious.
But because of the distinctive nature of its construction, the
organization also demands a quite different kind of responsibility and guidance — we termed it the power of the person.
The specific characteristics of this quality, as they are required
by the facts of the case, must now be pieced together to form a
cohesive picture.

Now, the main weight of responsibility in the organization
is obviously not evenly divided between these two forces, the
institution and the person. The great historical process that
produced and developed the organization pushed the main
responsibility from the institutional to the personal side. Organizations stand or fall today according to the measure, and
by the force, of personal responsibility operative in them. Of
course, the institutional setting can never be dispensed with;
no free and purely personal association can work and function
properly in the long run. But the institution is so constructed

in our society that it grows numb and lifeless if it reigns alone. It presupposes free personality, which must be present to give it life.

But as we piece together the essential features of personal responsibility we are at the same time bringing together the answers we found to our second question. For it became evident that the word "individualization" involves no more than an outward state of affairs — simply man's release from the all-embracing ties of the sacrosanct traditional regulations of the old stratified society. When these disintegrate, the true reality of human corporate life lies no longer in the supra-individual, institutional dimension, but in that which has been "individualized." But what is this individualized entity? Is it the individual? Indeed not. That is a concept too narrow to accommodate the facts that our survey has brought to light. Nothing but the concept of the person is adequate to the case. Thus the answers to both questions converge — into a comprehensive elucidation of what we have designated as "personal life" or "personal responsibility."

Let us again make our point of departure quite clear. It is not the *concept* of the "person." That concept has a long history, which has freighted it with a great many different and, in part, contradictory meanings. Hence, we can hardly use the word without further clarification, because it has become vague and indefinite. The history of the concept only confirms this lack of precision, and can offer us no help in our attempt to understand the present. Our starting point, therefore, is not the word but the thing itself. Embedded in the history of our institutions, and in these institutions as they exist today, is a certain relation to reality. In addition, the world of organizations contains certain indications of, and presuppositions for, a specific human attitude. The resulting configuration is what concerns us here, and we follow the normal use of language in referring to it with the word "person," in the hope that the indefinite but living concept will acquire content and clarity from the structure that can be shown to exist. Current usage with respect to "person" seems to betray a vague but keen sense of a profound reality of our world; and it will serve our purposes well to follow these structural indicators and raise to the level of consciousness that which is but vaguely felt.

The first and most important thing about this modern existence as person is that our social structures demand it. They do not posit or determine or define it, but they demand it. That is something fundamentally new, and it is peculiar to the organizational principle. All the old generally accepted orders, sanctified by religion and resting on long traditions, produced their own appropriate types and impressed their own stamp on them. That was so in medieval Christianity, although here Christian transcendence kept the patterns open and in principle left them in some doubt (one may think, for instance, of the Christian knight as he is portrayed in *Parsifal*). But in effect one could say of that period too that king and emperor, knight and priest, citizen and peasant were figures determined and shaped by their institutions, for the institution was the primary thing, in existence before the figures themselves, and it was as representatives of their class and rank that they were what they were. Something similar can be said even of "personality" in the sense of nineteenth-century idealism; it too acquired its distinctive quality, its standing, and its developed form only through sharing in a supraindividual "spirit," a realm of ideas, norms, and values that laid one under obligation.[1] It was this realm which placed its stamp on the individual and put him in living communication with other individuals of the same caliber.

The relationship of the organization to its members and representatives is quite different. It presupposes that there are forces which it can call upon and challenge, and it expects a vigorous personal response — these are just the forces and the response that we have described as personal. Thus the organization points beyond itself and the forces it controls to other forces which it needs for its own existence. If in the following pages we attempt to trace the shape of those forces, we shall

[1] See Ernst Michel, *Der Prozess Gesellschaft contra Person* (Stuttgart, 1959), p. 15.

not arrive at a replica of anything in the phenomenal world but at something suggested by the structures themselves and by that for which they are designed; it will be something that is indicated for the men within those structures.

As to its content, the structure of personal responsibility (as became evident in the preceding pages) falls naturally into three spheres: (1) relationship to the existing facts; (2) relationship to other people; and (3) relationship to oneself. As we discuss each of these in turn we shall see that each is demanded today, but in a specific form.

Objectivity

The demand for objectivity[2] includes the relationship to the existing facts. That will be readily agreed, but on closer examination the relationship demanded will be seen to be rich in meaning and to presuppose a great deal. Twenty-five centuries, if not a great many more, have been necessary to develop this relationship. Once again, Greek thought and Christian freedom from magical taboos stand at its point of origin, and a long time has been required to draw the conclusions that we accept today. This relationship is the one which was first openly proclaimed by the popes and was unheard of till then, namely, that one acts "as circumstances require." This radically changed the nature of political life, and finally caused the whole of the remaining world of tradition to wither away and collapse. The traditional orders and institutions had in some degree taken up a position between men and the facts. At that time life took its course mainly in well-known and predetermined situations, and law and custom dictated the exact ways in which recurring situations were to be met: work and the administration of justice; birth, marriage, and death; peace and war; overlordship and vassalage. Our organized institutions of today, however, allow man to take quite a different stance in the world. Their

[2] [*Sachlichkeit,* which means something like devotion to the issues or facts at hand; it and *sachlich* have been variously translated in preceding contexts, in order to bring out the specific connotations; for the sake of brevity *sachlichkeit* is here rendered "objectivity," which has some of the same connotations as the German word. — TRANS.]

great flexibility confronts him constantly with new and untried situations: political revolutions and reforms, military disasters, economic upheavals, technical inventions, population growth, large-scale influxes into the cities, and mass migrations to new lands, whether in flight or because of expulsion. All these things, on a larger or smaller scale, repeatedly surpass all our previous experience and compel us to find new means of dealing with new circumstances. This is what demands continued objectivity from us.

What exactly is the "thing" [*Sache*] on which objectivity focuses? In the first place it is the given facts of the case, the circumstances that confront us, at a given moment, in a particular combination, and set us the task of dealing with them: in the conduct of one's own life, in education, in the carrying out of one's work, in the representation of interests, in the political sphere. This combination of circumstances has many characteristics, of which we may single out for mention only three, since they have appeared repeatedly in the foregoing pages.

First, this set of circumstances is basically flexible, and although its component parts may be present for a long time and may even become painfully monotonous, change is always in the background, ready to break in at any time and confront one with new problems — problems which may or may not have been anticipated.

Secondly, the combination is basically unlimited. The great circulatory network of action and reaction may mean that even the remotest of circumstances may come to play a role, either directly or indirectly. At bottom, the modest personal affairs of the individual are determined by the hard realities of the world — the political, technological, economic, and intellectual facts. Moreover, this combination of circumstances embraces not only the present, but also a far-reaching historical past; that is why we have thought it necessary in earlier pages to discuss at least briefly the historical paths which have led to the present circumstances.

Lastly, this given set of facts is no neatly rounded-off unity, for the world of organizations is in its very essence pluralistic, which means that it contains facts and structures which not only cohere in the great circulatory network but may equally well stand brusquely side by side, and even remain in antagonism and logical contradiction. Thus, the existing set of circumstances turns out to be, on closer inspection, a jumble of criss-crossing facts.

If objectivity is to deserve the name, it must be able to cope with these three characteristics (there is no need to lengthen the list). Thus the constant possibility of change demands flexibility of judgment which will never rest content with fixed prejudices but will always be ready to reexamine and reconsider. The absence of any limit to the set of circumstances that one confronts demands an openness that will break through the narrowness of one-sided points of view, and will never refuse to expand its horizon, when that is called for. Finally, variety and contradiction demand intrepidity and the will to mastery, without which objectivity remains powerless.

However, we are not simply confronted with a set of circumstances as mere objects to be recognized and dealt with; nor are we as yet persons if we are merely subjects facing objects. At a given moment the set of circumstances will come to a head as my "situation," and that is an essential mark of my existence as a person. "A 'situation' is a set of circumstances that relates to persons and is colored according to their concerns."[3] Indeed, one has to put it more strongly: at times I *am* my situation, including all earlier situations, namely, my background and development. One way to acquire knowledge of a person today is through his *curriculum vitae*. There was a time when a man was what he was by virtue of his station in life. His station was his existence-in-the-world; it placed him with prescribed modes of conduct into situations that, as often as they recurred, were always the same. The modern world of organizations has placed man into open, changing situations, and so into a course of life that may take unexpected turns.

---

[3] C. A. Emge, *Über die Problematik im Begriffe der Situation* ("Abhandlungen der Preussischen Akademie der Wissenschaften," 1943, Phil.-hist. Klasse, No. 15 [Berlin, 1944]), p. 6.

Man's situation today is an open one, peculiar to the individual, in contrast to that of the man of yesterday, who had a fixed and immutable station in life. Today life gets its meaning and significance from the situation, and not, as in former times, from a social order that flourished far and wide; moreover, these are imparted in a different way. To perceive the meaning and significance in each particular instance is a function of the objectivity demanded by the existing structures, for only thus will the circumstances of the case be not only thought through but also experienced and appropriated as one's "situation." Only thus does objectivity fully become a personal quality. Objectivity is not merely something rational; besides understanding and reason it includes many, in fact all, of a person's faculties.

Thus one's relationship to the facts, and the objectivity that is adequate for that relationship, are self-contradictory: they are at once in opposition and in unity, separate and identical. And that is the only way, in this structural tension, that we are to understand what is said about "demanding." It is in such a way that objectivity is demanded of man in the modern world. The old order, too, made its demands; but it did so peremptorily, and at the same time it laid down in detail just how those demands were to be met. The open situation, on the other hand, calls on man to solve a problem in his own way, to respond in a way that may vary drastically from one case to the next but which, when the solution is a happy one, is seen to be the only possible one. The old order kept people in tutelage, whereas the open situation declares them to be of age. Man in the stratified society was governed by his institutions, however high his rank might be. The modern world of organizations, with its ever-new situations, demands a free man, and that means an objective man.

Partnership

Alongside one's relationship to the facts stands one's relationship to the other person, and just as objectivity is demanded for the former, so partnership is needed for the latter. In our usage of this word, too, we have to proceed, not from the word itself and the history of its meaning, but from the existing facts, and these may well be denoted by this word, which is in common use today.

In what we here call partnership, which is the relationship that our world of organizations requires us to adopt toward another person, we find the same dialectical structural principle at work as in the relationship to the facts, the relationship that we have called objectivity. In both cases there is at once a detached kind of encounter and a close mutuality, indeed, a unity; and the encounter presupposes that in principle those concerned meet on the same level. We may again refer to the observations made by Popitz[4] concerning highly mechanized work processes, observations which are — as he himself suggests — of general significance for life in the "industrial society." He speaks, it will be recalled, of an "unusual intensity of interdependence,"[5] which yet leaves people "in an unusual kind of detachment from one another."[6] As to the idea of a basic equality of status among modern men, even where a system of rank and command exist, such equality is fundamental to the structure of associations and federations; in politics it has been the source of all revolutions, and today it is asserting itself inexorably in the world of work as well. These manifold and irremovable contradictions — dependence and detachment, equality and rank — give to man's relationship to man in the present day the same marked tension that characterizes his relationship to the facts. Partnership and objectivity, if understood in this way, are concepts full of contradictions, which give them a peculiar elasticity and vigor, but also great precariousness and instability.

We need to go a little more deeply into these three factors of the partner relationship — isolation or detachment, interdependence, and equality. There is no doubt that modern man

---

[4] Heinrich Popitz, H. P. Bahrdt, E. A. Jüres, and H. Kesting, *Technik und Industriearbeit. Soziologische Untersuchungen in der Hüttenindustrie* (Tübingen, 1957).
[5] *Ibid.*, p. 188. (See p. 111 above.)
[6] *Ibid.*, p. 187. (See p. 111 above.)

is really a very solitary individual among other men, whether or not he realizes it and lives as such. That arises out of his "situation" in the sense described above, a situation that is in the last resort unique in any given case: peculiar to him alone among all other men, and now unique even as far as he himself is concerned, and never to recur in exactly the same way. No other person is involved in precisely the same set of institutions or has had the same sequence of experiences in the course of his life; the result is that, whatever his situation, it is very personal and peculiar to himself. That, indeed, is what makes it so difficult today to understand and advise people, because we can never entirely reproduce the other man's situation, even with the fullest information, the most unreserved disclosures, and the most affectionate empathy. For the same reason, "authority," in the old strict sense of existential compulsion exercised on the entire person, is no longer possible — assuming the requirements of a modern society built up strictly on the right lines. That has very practical consequences for the conduct of government and of business, or for the representation of another's interests. The person with whom we are faced can be understood, guided, and represented only on the periphery of his being; we have to regard him as impenetrable in his own right. All this keeps people today in an "unusual kind of detachment from one another," a detachment to which we are as yet unaccustomed, for it is new and not yet adequately understood and respected.

Alongside it, however, yet unconnected with it and in irreconcilable contradiction to it, stands the equally "unusual intensity of interdependence," the "detailed, exacting, and fatiguing dependence" in which we find ourselves everywhere. That, too, arises out of our experience of the "situation." For just as the situation isolates down to the last detail, it also unites at every point, and creates common ties that are no less real and effective than the isolating factors. To say that one is a citizen of a certain country, or in a certain line of work, or a member of a certain political party, or a taxpayer, is to say that one shares those situations with others. It is of the essence of organizations that they institutionalize such situations of common interests, or that they produce them and then cultivate them. The better and the more effectively they do this, the more stable is their structure.

The passage we have been citing from Popitz's study yields still further insights regarding common ties and interests in modern conditions. The interdependence observed by the investigators to be present among the workers presupposes "mutual trust and a levelheaded trustworthiness on the part of each individual . . . . As soon as one falls short of the necessary minimum of specific technical competence demanded by the situation, this is 'unsocial' behavior. But above this lower limit there emerges a kind of mutual appreciation . . . ."[7] Here in straightforward language based on an actual situation we are told that today situations create institutions, and we are told also how this comes about. If a situation is successfully mastered, there is "mutual appreciation," a typical characteristic of all institutions; if one's capacities are not equal to the demands placed on them, that is "unsocial behavior." However, "mutual trust" is an indispensable concomitant; it may be an unexpected requirement, but it is a very characteristic one in our modern world of technology and organizations. "The history of the modern economic system is the history of the development of trust," wrote the political economist Arthur Salz in 1930,[8] and that is true in all areas of modern life, not simply in economics. The complication of processes, the specialization of functions, the great network of action and reaction — all these make trust an essential condition of every sphere of life. The politician derives his authority from the trust of the electors; the businessman regards his customers' goodwill as nothing short of a calculable asset; and no doctor or lawyer or accountant can work without the trust of his patients or clients — "credit" is the vital nerve of all economic activity.

[7] *Ibid.*, p. 188. (See p. 111 above.)
[8] Arthur Salz, "Die irrationale Grundlage der kapitalischen Wirtschafts- und Gesellschaftsordnung," *Soziologische Studien zur Politik, Wirtschaft und Kultur der Gegenwart, Alfred Weber gewidmet* (Potsdam: Protte Verlag, 1930), pp. 56–57.

In the individual case, this trust always relates to a "level-headed trustworthiness on the part of each individual in his particular contribution to the effort as a whole"; it relates to "specific technical competence."[9] Anything more than these partial achievements will not concern us from one case to another, for, after all, we are living and acting in organizations. But, as was noted earlier, "every human response to the challenge of a particular situation contains a 'more' factor." The workers studied — and again this is of general application — "relate their particular part in the whole effort to their persons, and their response issues from the whole context of their lives, their capacities, and their energies, and it is therefore sometimes more than is asked of them."[10] In our organizations, therefore, we are never addressed more than "partially," but our response issues from our whole being. That is because the question proceeds from a "situation" that we ourselves have learned to know with our whole being.

In view of all this, it seems as if "unusual intensity of interdependence" does not adequately express the facts of the case. For neither in the mechanized work processes, the study of which led to the foregoing remarks, nor anywhere in the manifold contexts of the organization, is it the individual himself — not even the dependent individual — who does the job. This is true whether it be the boss or the worker, the board chairman or the chief executive, the plant manager or the director of sales, the foreman or the mechanic, indeed, the government worker or the citizen. The job is always done by the group in its entirety, by all of the participants taken as a whole. With respect to the goal envisioned and the situation in question, all of the people connected with the task constitute a unity, an "ensemble," and the really vital and uniting element in that unity is trust.

That, in brief, is the paradox that confronts us in the relationship of one person to another today: the basic individuality and solitariness and the equally basic dependence, and indeed unity, that are required from one case to the next by the facts

[9] Popitz *et al., op. cit.,* p. 188. (See p. 111 above.)
[10] *Ibid.,* pp. 176–77. (See p. 112 above.)

of a given situation, each party having fundamentally the same status and both considered "of age" in relation to the facts at hand. The word "partnership" seems an apt designation of such a relationship.

Responsibility for Oneself

The third relationship that is laid on us is that of a person to himself. This too comes in the form of a demand, one which can be briefly comprehended under one idea: the demand for responsibility for oneself. And this idea again is rich in meaning and laden with tension; in fact, it contains the same dialectical structural principle as the other two relationships: harmony and discord simultaneously among the elements of detachment, unity, and maturity.

As to detachment, anthropology has defined man as "the being that sees himself in perspective."[11] This characteristic, which distinguishes man from the animals, is evoked more by the world of organizations than by the world of traditional orders and institutions. Some writers have called attention to a particularly marked "self-critical" relationship of modern man to himself, a growing "eccentricity," that is, having an axis outside himself.[12] That is in the nature of the case. Earlier we observed that because only a part of one's personality belongs to a given organization, total surveillance of the institutional kind is impossible today — the kind that used to be commonly and indisputably exercised under the aegis of professional honor, ecclesiastical discipline, the commonweal, and so on. Today we find such surveillance intolerable, we will brook no "interference," and we think we know our own business best. But that means we are more than ready to accept something that is expected of us anyway — by virtue of the fact that things are as they are — namely, self-criticism and responsi-

[11] Arnold Gehlen, *Der Mensch. Seine Natur und seine Stellung in der Welt* (Berlin, 1941), p. 20.
[12] See Helmut Schelsky, "Über die Stabilität von Institutionen, besonders Verfassungen," *Jahrbuch für Sozialwissenschaft*, XLIV, No. 1 (1952), 15. Also Helmuth Plessner, *Die Stufen des Organischen und der Mensch. Einleitung in die philosophische Anthropologie* (Berlin: De Gruyter, 1928).

bility for oneself. The modern world demands of us that we take a detached and critical attitude toward ourselves, observe our thoughts and actions, and render an account of them. The true center of responsibility is no longer in the supraindividual institution, but in ourselves. Once again, this means that an element of precariousness and instability is introduced into our world, for, if we have understood the new relationship aright, there are no longer any guarantors of responsibility. If everyone can and will guarantee only his own responsibility, who is going to guarantee the guarantors? But uncertainty is increased by the fact that even for well-disposed people aware of their responsibility the standards of judgment have grown uncertain. For the standards that society has inherited and worked out are still those of the institutional norms of traditional modes of conduct. But the standards of responsibility for self that are adequate to meet present-day requirements lie in the relationships of objectivity and partnership in the senses indicated earlier. Here the general social consciousness has not yet come to terms with the new situation.

To be able to take a critical stance toward oneself is only half of the story, however. If self-criticism dominates unchecked, the personality is split and loses self-confidence and the capacity for action. So here again there must be unity, which, of course, is a different kind of unity from that imposed by the old stratified society, which gave us the clear profiles of figures like the knight, the merchant prince, the citizen of the Greek city, the monk. What is needed today is unaffected freedom that is able to coexist with self-criticism and to sustain all the tensions and contradictions of objectivity and partnership. If one is inclined to keep or reapply the old notion of "unpretentiousness" as a mode of conduct, it will have to be much broader in conception and different in content.

In this responsibility for oneself, as in objectivity and partnership, a stance commensurate with being "of age" is essential. One's freedom in unity with oneself is compatible with self-criticism only if that criticism does not merely involve severely disciplining and keeping in check the "old Adam,"

157

the rogue within us. We also have to watch carefully our own growth and give it play if our introspection is to lead to a maturing process.

That is how we may perhaps sketch the kind of attitude that society as now constituted demands of us, and what we mean here by "being a person." We stand in tension and paradox before the facts of the case and in our "situation" — we have called this "objectivity." We lead a solitary life alongside the other person, yet are at the same time inextricably bound to him — we have called this "partnership." Finally, there is the necessary self-criticism, which, however, must not end in paralyzing self-analysis, but must lead to unaffected freedom of action — we have called this "responsibility for oneself." All this assumes that persons "come of age" with a maturity that will tolerate no tutelage but insists on standing on its own in relation to the facts, to the other person, and to oneself.

These three attitudes are intimately related to each other; they are not required of us one at a time, now here, now there; they are all constantly involved simultaneously. There is no objectivity without partnership, and vice versa, if we take them both in the strict sense. And both are constantly built up on a self-criticism that is capable of effective action.

Conversation

All three requirements, intimately united, can be seen at first hand in a social activity in which we are constantly engaged, and which may rightly be regarded as a basic constituent of modern society: conversation. Conversation is a homely and transient form of social intercourse which can always be resumed intact and which may be demanded of us at any time. Its structural elements are precisely those which, as we have seen, are needed in our own time for conduct as a person: here two or more people meet out of, and in, their various situations and have to maintain their positions; at the same time they have in common a situation that produces the material for their conversation, and to whose solution they are to contribute, each from his own position. As they do so, this common obligation in relation to the matter under discussion puts them essentially on an equal footing; without this equality of status their talk would scarcely deserve to be called "conversation." It is clear that for conversation to be successful the attitudes required are, again, the personal kind: frank and flexible objectivity; the recognition of the other person as an independent and yet related "partner" in conversation; and lastly a responsibility for oneself that is capable of combining self-criticism with self-confidence. It is no accident that the concept of a "dialectical" structural principle suggested itself earlier in these pages as applicable to the constantly reappearing association of remoteness, unity, and equal status.

Closely connected with what we have been saying is the fact that conversation is becoming increasingly important in the modern world, and that refusal to make use of it leads to grave dislocations and conflicts, irritations and disappointments. When we discussed the three forms of organization — federation, business, and state — and again in our discussion of their integration, it was everywhere obvious that the modern world is not accustomed to unilateral decisions but demands instead objective discussion among the people concerned, so as to reach solutions that represent a consensus. And so in the modern world conversation assumes the most varied forms — there are negotiations, conferences, discussions, conventions, congresses, interviews. But even forms of communication which used to be rather one-sided now tend more and more to approach the form of dialogue — they are compelled to do so if they are to be effective. All counsel misses its mark if it does not issue from a mutual discussion of the questions at issue, whether in a medical consultation, a technical conference, or whatever. For some decades now pedagogy has moved resolutely toward the conversational method of teaching. In industry, the more complicated a job, the less it is possible to issue unilateral commands. Today lectures and sermons are all the more effective if they are regarded, and are meant to be regarded, as conversations with the audience. In fact, in World War II even the military command, which was once looked on as the strictest unilateral pronouncement, repeatedly had to be couched, even among the lowest ranks, in the form of an objective conversation about how and when it was to be carried out. It is therefore no exaggeration to say, as we did at the start, that conversation must be regarded as a basic constituent of modern society. Conversation is the functional manifestation of existence as a person, and existence as a person is what the modern world demands for the sake of its own stability.

10

The Personal Society

in Danger

The Fragility of the Modern World

In the foregoing reflections we have had to stress repeatedly that the development from the old orders to modern organizations, the shifting of responsibility from institutions to persons, has brought the world into a very precarious state. Our age is only too well aware of this precariousness. We see it in the uncertainty that the world feels every day in great things as well as in small. It erupted in the catastrophes of recent decades, and it may do so again repeatedly. It is man's "thrownness,"[1] which, significantly enough, existential philosophy has seen and articulated in our own time.

Now it is in order, and indeed necessary, that we devote a special chapter to emphasizing most strongly this fragility of modern existence. Only thus can we avoid the mistake of supposing that our remarks about personal responsibility have been concerned with practical instructions that need only be faithfully followed out in order that a new age of stability and

[1] [In rendering *Geworfenheit* (or *Geworfensein*) as "thrownness," we are following Werner Brock (see his introduction to Martin Heidegger's *Existence and Being*, trans. Douglas Scott *et al.* [Chicago: Henry Regnery Co., 1949], pp. 34 ff.) and Reginald H. Fuller (see his translation of H. W. Bartsch [ed.] *Kerygma and Myth* [London: S. P. C. K., 1953], p. xi). — TRANS.]

security may be ushered in. Nothing could be further from the truth.

That is clear if we examine some reasons why society is in a precarious state. In the first place, the modern organizational structure of society has created such a radically new situation that the new modes of conduct are still largely unknown, or at any rate untested, and have not yet been generally adopted. It will be a long time before that happens; but at the end of that time we might be able to promise ourselves a new stability.

This, however, is less true of the second reason, the fact that modern society does not shape and stamp the man whose nature is commensurate with it; it merely makes its demands. And the right way of responding, one based on an attitude commensurate with the structure of modern society, remains uncertain, since it always has to be discovered afresh.

In the third place, however — and this is a very serious point — our picture of personal responsibility, as it has emerged from the given facts, displays unmistakably utopian features — features which do not accord with the nature of historical man and which impose upon him demands so high that he cannot fully comply with them on the strength of his own resources. For that is how things stand with regard to the demand that, in principle, we set no limits in our judgment of the circumstances of a case, recognizing that in the great circulatory network of modern life everything is in some way or other affected by a person's actions. Fortunately we do not often experience this in everyday life, though, for instance, the politicians of the world soon come up against the limits of human possibilities: today one simply cannot take everything into account and think out in advance all the consequences of one's actions. The same is true also of the demand for complete openness to new insights, and for readiness always to reconsider previous judgments. The demand is not to be disputed, but who can comply with it? One's existing judgments are the fruit of decades of growth and experience; they are not to be revised on short notice. We live within a structure of ideas and concepts that is more rigid than our flexible situations demand.

162

And finally, to touch on one other point, the equal status of all men, which we are required to acknowledge and which is irrevocably anchored in our legal codes, is in contradiction to all actual experience. Real equality of status is never more than a marginal and exceptional phenomenon. Occupational and social position, age and experience, learning and natural gifts, and a great deal besides, almost always create a configuration that makes the theoretical equality of status appear artificial and unreal. These features cannot, in the last resort, receive full recognition in practice; in the historical realm they will always fall far short of any complete or certain realization.

Furthermore, if we reflect that responsibility is being shifted increasingly from the institution to the person, we must also assume that the precariousness of our world will continue to grow. Mankind is being drawn into a situation in which the demands are becoming increasingly stringent and overwhelming and always more difficult to meet. This fragile and problematical nature of our world has long been the subject of keen criticism. A considerable literature is bringing to our notice, persistently and urgently, the nature and extent of the danger.

A number of ideas that crop up most frequently in this connection are derived from the concept of the "mass." Our age is called the "age of the mass" — mass production, mass psychology, mass burials, and so on. The trend is said to be toward a general "massification" of life. "The mass is becoming absolute," observed Goethe many years ago in a notation made for a sequel to his drama dealing with revolution and the future, *Die natürliche Tochter*. In that word "mass," which is not always used clearly or precisely, converge all the anxieties and laments about our age, which still eludes our mastery.

The "Secondary System"

In his *Theorie des gegenwärtigen Zeitalters*[2] Hans Freyer has rendered a useful service by giving this critique of our cul-

---

[2] Hans Freyer, *Theorie des gegenwärtigen Zeitalters* (Stuttgart: Deutsche Verlags-Anstalt, 1955).

ture clear and concise expression; in doing so he subjects the concepts of the "mass" and "massification" to critical examination. He fits them into a comprehensive concept of his own which he has termed the "secondary system." By this he means much the same as what we understand here by the social world of organizations. In his presentation and criticism of the "secondary system" our organizational world appears as problematical and fragile, as a social setting that has not been mastered.

Since the publication of Freyer's book the concept of the "secondary system" has become common coin, especially in ecclesiastical pronouncements. For that reason, and because Freyer presents the situation in sharp outline, we may be allowed to take up here some of his characterizations of the dangers to our society. As we do so it will also become evident what direction future discussion of his book should take.

Freyer's "secondary system" is the world of organizations when it regards itself as absolute and has failed to perceive the law of its own life and growth. This is the organization as institution; it does not see its own finite nature and its dependence on forces that lie outside it, and it believes it can still apprehend and direct the whole of a person's life, as the old orders and institutions used to do. There is no doubt that this idea was dominant in the early days of the organization, that even today people everywhere are laboring under it, and that here the "mentality of modern natural science" has the upper hand in the social sphere: "As it is thought there, so we build here." The "secondary system" is "held to be capable of being thought out to the last degree," and therefore "equally capable of being guided and changed at will." "Everything that goes into this structure" is to be "provided for in the blueprint and set going on its own power, and only the elements planned for it are to play any part in it." "Man is . . . reduced to a minimum. He becomes . . . one element equipped with any qualities that may be indicated."[3] "What he is is decided, not of his own accord, but by his position and function in the factual

[3]*Ibid.*, p. 83.

process . . . . That is exactly how a 'proletarian' is thought of: a man who has been so completely subsumed under a factual system that any motive powers that arise in himself do not now become operative . . . ."[4] "For the secondary system grips, normalizes, and proletarianizes a man, not only as a fellow worker, but equally as a fellow consumer . . . ."[5] "Adaptation is one of the obligatory ways of behaving in such a social structure,"[6] but adaptation to the secondary system is "a real danger."[7]

In these characteristics, which Freyer has formulated in general terms, we shall have little difficulty in recognizing all those types of people who provoke criticism today: the "bureaucrat" who simply sees "cases" without regard to the life situation; the "functionary" who is subservient to his federation and lacks the courage or capacity to judge for himself; the "fanatic" for whom one particular slice of the world, presented to him by his ideology, contains the whole truth, and who never gets as far as a balanced objective judgment; the "naïve" person who is at home in his own particular sphere but cannot take up a critical attitude that necessitates breadth of view; the "dictator" in business, in administration, or on a board of directors, who thinks he is the only one who knows anything, wants to do everything himself, and simply expects his orders to be carried out to the letter without regard to anything that may be said by his subordinates or those affected by the orders; and last but not least the "totalitarian state," of which Freyer rightly says, "Totalitarianism is the particular danger of secondary systems,"[8] for only totalitarian systems deliberately set about to diminish man.[9]

As the antitype to this diminished and adapted man, Freyer sees man in "all those social orders that predominated and were held to be valid in town and country, in society and state,

[4] *Ibid.*, p. 89.
[5] *Ibid.*, p. 91.
[6] *Ibid.*, p. 97.
[7] *Ibid.*, p. 238.
[8] *Ibid.*, p. 169.
[9] *Ibid.*, p. 170.

till the dawn of the industrial age."[10] These are the old traditional, religiously sanctioned orders of the stratified society —
those orders which sustained not only the West in the Middle
Ages, but all peoples before the modern world either emerged
from those peoples or took hold of them from outside. In these
orders, and in their legacy, Freyer sees the only substance that
seems to offer the possibility of mastering the perilous new
world; in them, too, he finds the reliable yardstick by which
the new world can and must be measured. This legacy must be
preserved within the new order, for he sees in "progress and
persistence the two ways in which history 'breathes'; they stimulate and vindicate each other."[11] The opponents of progress
are "those who, of set purpose, belong to yesterday," who "re-
tain as many of its structures and orders as possible . . . even if
it is as foreign bodies between the building blocks of the secondary system . . . ."[12] In these "conserving powers and their
agents" Freyer sees the possibility of preventing the plunge into
brutality that would be the final result of the "secondary system." His sets his hope on the type of the "conservative revolutionary and reformer — in the whole spectrum from Augustus
to Cromwell."[13]

These formulas of "progress and persistence" and "conserving powers" no doubt denote inherent laws of history. They
were especially applicable, however, to the first period of the
industrial upheaval, in the nineteenth and early twentieth
centuries. Here new structures came tumbling forth in a tor-
rent, and the people who created and shaped them were carried
over and past all obstacles and initial uncertainties by their
intoxicating faith in future progress. There were indeed voices
raised in opposition, giving expression to the acute anxiety
about a precious ancient legacy, about the cultivation of virtues
that had taken hundreds of years to acquire and were badly
needed to meet new and untried conditions, if everything was

[10] *Ibid.*, p. 85.
[11] *Ibid.*, 240. ["Persistence," which renders *Beharrung*, is used in the sense
of "lasting," "enduring." — TRANS.]
[12] *Ibid.*, p. 239.
[13] *Ibid.*, p. 240.

not to go to pieces in a lax do-as-you-please atmosphere. So the universal law of history, that progress and persistence should go hand in hand, marked this era of the great upheaval in a particularly acute and comprehensive way, and Freyer's analysis of it is fascinating and cogently formulated.

Freyer's book is thus a farewell to that era. Rightly considered, it is not a theory of the present age, as the title suggests, but a liberating summation of an age that has passed, the sort of summing up that always has to be carried through when we have to recognize and clear the way for the beginning of a new path into the future. Not that Freyer's portraits of the adapted and diminished man are no longer correct. They are still an oppressive reality, as they were before. And our age is still gratefully conscious, with Freyer, of the supporting strength of "conserving powers," which live on the heritage of old times and old orders. Such support is to be cherished: chivalry, patriotism, integrity in government, rural life, honest workmanship, traditions of the "merchant prince," European scholarship, and much besides — these things live on in our world and count for more than we are apt to suppose. The real issue now, however, is not "Progress or persistence?" or even "How can progress exist side by side with persistence?" but rather that something new is coming into being. We are beginning to realize that the basic aim of the organizational world is not the adapted or diminished man, but the "person." It was a mistake when, in the early days of the industrial world, it was supposed that a completely rational "secondary system," cut adrift from all historical moorings, could exist, like a sacrosanct ordering, in its own self-sufficiency. The more the world of organizations developed, the more clearly it saw that it had to rely on forces and resources outside itself, beyond what can be fashioned or reasoned, and beyond any functional design. For a long time those forces stemmed mainly from tradition and the legacy of the past. Hans Freyer has conclusively and accurately described the tension of their interplay with the "organization." But side by side with these forces are others that have also been operative from the very outset, and it is to these that the

stress has shifted as the organization has matured; we have
called them "personal" forces. What is crucial today for mastering the world of organizations is no longer the retention of the
heritage — it plays only a supportive role — but a firm grasp
of what is new and, at the same time, is the result of a long
historical development.

At the end of his analysis, even Freyer sees the possibility
"that some time or other a human basis may be added to the
secondary system,"[14] and elements of that basis are discernible
in his book at a number of points. He shows, for example, that
the person has an unassailable existence outside the system:
"Man does not cease to be a person if he is socialized. It is as a
person that demands are placed upon him, and in the extreme
case it is as a person that he becomes estranged. That is no
postulate in the liberal, individualist, or humanist sense, but a
structural fact."[15] He further shows the person as the supporting force of the institution: "All community is embodied in
persons . . . . Man's freedom is the abutment by which community is shored up . . . . It is possible to reduce this pole to a
minimum. That, basically, is what the secondary systems
do . . . . Whether that is completely possible, or possible in
the long run, is a question we shall have to ask later."[16] Freyer
also detects that dialectical relationship between the person
and the situation which we have seen to be characteristic of
modern man's relationship to reality: "What does it mean to be
equal to a situation? One first has to step onto its own plane
and become involved with it; otherwise one does not even
meet it, but simply passes it by . . . . But one must have something with which to counter, something to bring to bear, at
points where there is a deficiency. One must have some support
and stay in relation to the situation, or some freedom of
maneuver; otherwise one is submerged in it and has no existence apart from it. Related and unrelated, joined as opponents
are joined to each other, and free as the living person is as long

[14] *Ibid.*, p. 245.
[15] *Ibid.*, p. 160.
[16] *Ibid.*, p. 159.

as he does not abandon himself and his cause: this duality exists even in the simplest case where a man is equal to a situation."[17]

Like the interplay of persistence and progress, this relationship of the person to the institution and to the situation is also put forward by Freyer as a universal historical law — and that, in fact, is what they both are. But at the same time both themes are leitmotifs from a different era. The period of early industrialism was above all a struggle between the new and the old, between "forces of movement" and "forces of persistence,"[18] between future aspiration and conservative retention of the old. Another epoch, our own, has already begun, in which organizations are part of the landscape; and the leitmotif now is the developing consciousness of the person in and alongside the organization, in and before the situation. Thus Freyer's analysis characterizes a significant turning point in our history; he balances the ledger for one epoch, and he looks forward to a new and different era.

Totalitarian States

In this chapter about the threats to our time we must refer briefly to the totalitarian state, that "particular danger of secondary systems," to recall Freyer's words. The characteristic of the totalitarian regime is "the unbridled takeover of the organs of power and the complete enthronement of the state mechanism."[19] What does that mean in the context of our present discussion?

Put briefly, it means that an organization lays claim to the comprehensive and unconditional validity that was once accorded to a sacrosanct order of things. But that is to mix two historically distinct types of institution, and such a mixture cannot be maintained in the long run. For the totalitarian state is an organization through and through. That is, it tries to carry through to its utter logical conclusion the tendency of the

[17] *Ibid.*, pp. 234–35.
[18] Wilhelm Heinrich Riehl, *Die bürgerliche Gesellschaft* (Stuttgart: Verlag Cotta, 1861), pp. 49, 243.
[19] Freyer, *op. cit.*, pp. 169–70.

modern state toward a flexible and calculated pursuit of its goals. But at the same time it labors to revive absolute authority, which has been shed in proportion as objectivity has advanced. Thus it becomes an organization that tries to solve everything along institutional lines and that attempts to bring the person back under a sacrosanct tutelage. It does not realize that objectivizing, desacralizing, and personalizing are indissolubly connected and must react on each other. A dictator in an advanced industrial society claims the sole right to all personality, just as the seventeenth- and eighteenth-century rulers did. But the latter had under them a nation that lived in the setting of "households" and traditional institutions. That old system of folk orders and institutions has been replaced by modern society with its great circulatory network of actions and reactions and, consequently, by a universal demand for freedom, that is, freedom to be a person. Everyone now *wants* to be a person because he *must* be a person. And so the person's will to be free in an industrial state is — to quote Hans Freyer once more — "no postulate in the liberal . . . or humanist sense, but a structural fact." Totalitarianism is absence of personality, and at the very point where society as presently constituted demands its presence. A totalitarian regime is therefore not of itself a danger in the first place; it is dangerous because it has drawn the logical consequences of the failure of personal responsibility. At the beginning of the twentieth century Russia was still an empire, in which collectivism and excessive authority gave no scope to the development of personality among the population as a whole. So a totalitarian dictatorship took the reins and in a few decades made good a century of neglect in education and industrialization. Today the Soviet rulers are confronted with a result that they did not expect; people with education want to bear, and must bear, independent personal responsibility in relation to the complicated problems of modern society. "What a kolkhoz [Russian collective farm] achieves depends entirely on its chairman," Krushchev himself once said.

170

The German totalitarian state was the danger with which the Weimar Republic was threatened and to which it succumbed when it was suffocated in a collection of ideologies, when political objectivity wilted, and the class and party struggle ignored the principle of partnership. General signs of the times were uncritical naïveté, ideological fanaticism, and dictatorial claims. Personal responsibility did not achieve what the situation demanded of it, and the upshot was that the person was completely eliminated and the institution ruled supreme. The collapse of 1945 made it possible to restore to the person his rightful status. We have now learned from experience that the threat to personality does not occur only in a full-blown totalitarian regime, but is a much more widespread danger. Totalitarianism in all its forms is the peculiar danger of the organizational world, and the omnipotence of the state's machinery is only the last and most extreme form of that danger, as far as our present experience will allow us to judge.

The danger is not simply that people who are opposed to freedom on principle may assault an unresisting world, but even more that personal responsibility may actually be felt to be oppressive and overwhelming in its demands, so that people will flee into the comfortable or supposedly more comfortable realm of a "sacrosanct-organizational" existence. People think they have discovered how feeble the person is, and so they want to recommit themselves to the power of the institution. But sooner or later a further experience is bound to come: personal freedom, however unstable and precarious, however tender and vulnerable, is in the long run much more powerful than the most powerful organization, if the latter tries to live solely on its own resources. There is no going back to the prepersonal age — that is the strange experience gleaned from an historical chain of events that have passed through the fires of judgment. We cannot retreat from the organization into the old sacrosanct orders, and the organization has its own inherent laws, which we can defy only at the price of ultimate disaster.

11

The Family as the Place

of the Person

The public social realm of our world can be reduced, as we have seen, to three basic types: the business and the association, both of which are without a doubt organizations, and the state with its establishments, which is more and more assuming such a character. In their midst, however, is another social entity, the family, more numerous than all the rest. It is certainly no "organization." So far we have mentioned it only incidentally, but now it is time to ask about its form, its role, and its significance in our world. How does the phenomenon of today's family fit into the picture that we have drawn here, and in what respect does it supplement it?

People like to regard the family as a timeless social entity, on the ground that the relationship of the sexes, procreation, birth, and the rearing of progeny are preordained in man's nature, and that, in the family, history is borne along on a current that flows unceasingly, without regard to historical conditions and beneath the changing historical events. Up to a point this is no doubt true, but only in a very limited sense. The pattern of marriage — the difference in the functions of man and wife and in the relative position of authority occupied by each, the way in which children are reared or life is safeguarded, the size of the family group and the kinds of laws that govern it, and much more besides — may take the most varied forms; and the form the family assumes at any particular time is largely dependent on historical circumstances and is an essential component of larger social configurations as these are shaped by history. That was true in the past, and it is true also of the family in its present form; and so the great upheaval that displayed its full force in the nineteenth century affected the pattern, not only of work, politics, and law, but also of the family. It meant that the family underwent a profound change of structure, and this took a form and direction that were entirely in line with the changes in other spheres of life.

The two terms used for the ideally typical pattern of the family before and after the upheaval were mentioned earlier in the section entitled "The Basic Types of the New Order."[1] Previously one lived in the "household," or, more accurately, the "whole household"; today one lives in the "family," or, more precisely, the modern "small family." The word "family" comes from the Latin *familia;* in German the word did not come into general use until the nineteenth century, simultaneously with the development and general adoption of the new pattern. It can be seen, therefore, that the supposedly timeless "family" is a phenomenon of a particular period in history, namely, our own.

Like the "household," the "family" has a distinctive part to play in our time; it has become, though in a quite different way, what the household once was — the keystone of the world about it. The medieval world was built on its households and their resources; the modern social world lives on its families and their resources.

Organizational Features

We must first realize that, although the "family" is certainly not an "organization," it has important features of an organization; and here it contrasts sharply with the older "household."

[1] Pp. 65–73 above.

The prototype and the commonest form of the household throughout the Middle Ages and into the nineteenth century was the farm, a largely self-contained entity designed for permanence. Every fresh marriage simply added a new link to an old chain, and everyone who was added by birth or marriage or by entering service there was admitted to an already existing traditional order to which he was expected to subject himself. So the household could be the type of an *ordo* in the strict sense, which would always be restored if it went awry.

The modern family is quite a different matter. Taken singly, it is not now a long-lived "order," but a highly mobile and changeable entity. When a couple get married today, they "start a family," a very significant and revealing expression. With each marriage something new comes into being, different from anything that existed before (we may recall what was said earlier about the "situation"), and this demands adventurous courage and inventive energy. And after the family has been started it passes through one new phase after another. There are changes of occupation or of location (so frequent today). Children are born and grow up. These phases demand a constant inventiveness and readiness to meet new situations. Finally the children leave home, which is no longer a "household" but a dwelling place; the parents are alone again, and when their lives are over, the family they started is extinguished, its place taken by others. The modern family is an extremely plastic entity, and in this respect it is very closely related to the organization.

There is still another correspondence between the family and the surrounding world of organizations. The lives of the individual members are not lived wholly within the family, any more than they are within the business and the association. Only the preschool children live in exactly the same setting as the mother. As soon as they start school, the children enter into a sphere of activities of which the parents can no longer fully keep track; and when, later on, they join clubs and make friends, their experience widens and leaves its particular impress on them. The same is true of marriage. However keenly a wife may share in her husband's concern for his work, it remains his own world, into which even his life partner can never fully enter. Alongside her own sphere, the family, she is usually in closer touch with the neighbors and relatives than is her husband, who is out at work — assuming that she does not work outside the home herself. Thus it is a fact common to the family and to the organizational world in which it exists that neither (in contrast to the earlier "household") absorbs the whole of its members' lives. The breakup of the household came about simply because the new organizations took over its tasks one by one, the first and most important being daily work. The family shares with the organizations a dual characteristic: it is not only an entity apart, unique and set off from its environment, but it is also open to all sides and closely interrelated with other entities. So we find the family as a member of the organizational world and closely joined to it through sharing some of the latter's important characteristics.

Three Basic Personal Relationships

On the other hand, it is equally plain that the family is not an organization but an entity apart, distinct and unique; and as such it occupies a place in the organizational world so important that it could never completely be replaced.

By that we mean more than just the truism that the family is the source of new life, and that the world of organizations would necessarily become extinct if there were no more births and rearing of children. We are stressing rather that the family is the place where the person as such can find a basis for his life and the conditions necessary for his existence, and where he can grow up into his own particular individuality. The organization makes demands on a person, but it does not contain him. The tasks it sets him are always parts of a larger whole, and while he must execute them (as we have seen) out of the "whole context of his life, his capacities, and his energies," this total context is really not what the organization is concerned about; rather, it is tacitly assumed. Indeed, this "total context" has even severer demands made on it inasmuch as in it resides the capacity to integrate the pluralistic world of organizations, as we saw in chapter eight. The fragmenting forces and conflicts of modern society threaten to carve a man up and dismember him; not only is he compelled to defend himself against that danger, but, by making his own integration secure, he must effect the integration of those divergent and conflicting forces.

Somewhere, then, in this organized society, the person himself must be made the subject of concern and must be nurtured and cherished. This applies in principle to all the members of society, for all have severe demands placed upon them. That "somewhere" is in the family, specifically, in the modern family. The old traditional "household" could not achieve this, for it was an *ordo,* primarily an institution and the central social structure of an age when men looked to the institution for guidance.

It is the unique and new structural significance of the modern family that it is based on personal relationships, and is therefore the place, par excellence, of personal existence. Elsewhere only demands are placed on a person — he cannot exist simply in his own right.

To illustrate this, we may refer once more to Popitz's characterization of conduct in the work process in industry, which he himself says is of general application. The connecting bond within the framework of the organization can and must be that of "trust." But trust is mediated and confirmed by sound performance. A man's performance is the source of recognition and trust.

The ties within the framework of the family are different. Here too, of course, there is "performance": meals must be prepared, and food, clothing, and housing secured. A family suffers severely when there is any persistent failure in these respects. But they are not the heart of the matter. That is found in the unconditional and ready acceptance of the other person, an acceptance that can become the source of all achievement and will not evaporate if the other person fails in achievement or is even at fault and therefore held in contempt by the outside world. In the family the essential thing is "love" — love between husband and wife, parents and children, and brothers and sisters. This love, which is independent of success or failure, is shown in a way that outsiders often cannot understand — in a wife's loyalty to her drunken husband or to her incurably sick child. In Ernst Wiechert's story "The Father"[2] a miner's widow says to her son who is about to leave for military service in the First World War, "My son, if you bring me honor I shall be proud of you, and if you bring me dishonor I shall always be your mother." That is how it is. What matters in the family is not the capacity for achievement, which is tacitly presupposed elsewhere, but the person himself.

But in the way in which the modern family lives out and fosters these personal relationships there appears the same dialectical structure that we observed in relationships on the job: there is emphasis on unity, on detachment, and on a tendency toward equal status. This holds good for all three relationships within the family — between husband and wife, parents and children, brothers and sisters. In the great social upheaval that took place mainly in the nineteenth century these relationships underwent a profound change, with a shifting of the stress from the traditional and institutional, and one's station in life, to the personal. The change consisted precisely in the development of these three characteristic features.

In former times the choice of the marriage partner was a matter for the household and the kinship as a whole, because it was necessary to ensure the continuity of the house. And in the case of the woman who was to enter the kinship through marriage, the important thing was not so much her personal qualities as whether she came from a suitable house, which would be regarded as an adequate guarantee of her character. Thus it was a case, not of a man's choosing a personal life partner, but of an institution's receiving a new member. In conformity with this, there was a measured formality in the married

---

[2] Ernst Wiechert, "Der Vater," *Die Novellen und Erzählungen* (Vienna: Kurt Desch-Verlag, 1962), pp. 477 ff.

couple's mutual relationship, as expressed in their speaking to each other using the polite form of address and in the authority that the husband exercised over his wife no less than over the rest of the household.

In the nineteenth century, however, there came increasingly into favor the "love match" based on the partner's personal choice, in support of which any consideration of the bride's "suitable" origin might — but need not — be added. The romantic novels of that time would repeat with infinite variations the conflict between personal affection and loyalty to one's station in life, a theme that is now relegated to articles on the royal families in the tabloids. Otherwise, however, in today's novels as well as in real life, the love match is taken for granted, although "love" may often be watered down to mean nothing more than inclination or infatuation. In any case, marriage, like the family generally, has become a thing of intimacy and privacy, a sphere closed off to those outside.

In strict and striking contrast to the married couple's intimate personal union is their corresponding separation in outside activities. Just when the love match was becoming the normal thing, the man's and the woman's spheres of life split off from each other. The man now left his family when he went to his work or attended to many other matters that used to be dealt with in the domestic circle. Since then, neither husband nor wife has been able completely to participate in the world of the other, as the duties of each are no longer shared on a continuing basis. There are many wives — the wife of a coal miner, for instance — who have never as much as seen their husband's place of employment.

Here, too, this dialectical tension of unity and remoteness is joined by a third factor: the tendency to equal rights. In West Germany, much legislation is directed toward implementing the equality of the sexes which is guaranteed by the constitution. But in this respect the law is merely following in the wake of a development that has been underway for a long time in family life, not least as a result of the two world wars. Sociological studies of the family by Helmut Schelsky and

Gerhard Wurzbacher have brought to light the "shifting of authority within the family toward the wife, and the increased claims made on her in the public sphere."[3] This has brought to married life an "image of equal status,"[4] which already seems to be predominant and gaining still further ground.

It almost goes without saying that in a marriage based on this dialectical principle dialogue itself plays an important part. Wurzbacher notices as one of the "most important stabilizing factors [in marriage] . . . the ability to exchange views . . . . 'All the questions that crop up are talked over together' . . . . With this increasing ability to exchange views, understanding assumes a greater importance; it now takes the edge off many disputes, as their causes and consequences can be seen more clearly. This represents a stabilizing factor, which is not in opposition to the demand for a deep personal relationship between the partners and can even be the expression of a more conscious mental and spiritual understanding . . . ."[5]

Like the relation between husband and wife, that between parents and children has been fundamentally altered during the transition from household to modern family. Here, too, a traditional authority of the institutional kind has become a dialectical personal relationship. Today children no longer address their father as "Sir," as though his were an undisputed traditional regime. The familiar terms of address express the unity of parents and children. Each of the latter may expect individual consideration, encouragement, and instruction. But at the same time the modern world, with its kindergartens, compulsory education, and youth clubs, has already provided the child at an early age with a world of his own outside the family, which creates an increasing detachment alongside the more intimate relationship. This detachment is the institutional opportunity for independent development, which again has made it possible for the children in many modern families to gain a

[3] Helmut Schelsky, *Wandlungen der deutschen Familie in der Gegenwart* (2d ed.; Stuttgart, 1954), p. 290.
[4] Gerhard Wurzbacher, *Leitbilder gegenwärtigen deutschen Familienlebens* (2d ed.; Stuttgart, 1954).
[5] *Ibid.*, p. 114.

marked degree of independence in relation to their parents, an independence that may actually grow into comradeship. There is a sound reason for this. Today every child is growing up towards his own majority under the law and his own personal responsibility, whereas formerly most grownups had to spend their lives under the legal authority of a *paterfamilias*. Wurzbacher thinks the image of the child's independence is gaining ground, and, significantly, his studies have revealed it to be almost always connected with marriages where husband and wife stood on an equal footing.[6] Anyone who treats his spouse as a "partner" is likely to respect the rights of his children, including the right to their own development; he is apt to refrain from trying to guide and mold them forcibly according to his own wishes. In both respects this attitude is in harmony with the realities of the modern world.

What has been said here also applies to the third relationship within the family: that between brothers and sisters. Here, too, there has been simultaneous growth in intimacy and in differentiation and detachment, the latter two as a result of each one's individual associations and development. Such differentiation is in harmony with the basically almost unlimited freedom to choose one's occupation from the great variety that now exists. In the world of the stratified society, on the other hand, the number of available occupations at any particular time was very limited. Here again the modern world, by abolishing the arbitrary privileges of the heir of the household, has moved toward equality of rights among brothers and sisters.

Taken all in all, we see in the family today an entity which of course has institutional rules and regulations — but these do not constitute the family's real life. The latter consists rather in a network of personal relationships in which the emphasis at any particular time is on the person himself and on his own individual life. And that life pursues its course in a dialectical relationship of intimate association, detached individuality, and essential equality of status.

[6] *Ibid.*, pp. 216–17.

A Base of Support for Organizations

In the days of the stratified society, everyone had to belong to a "household" in order to have a place in the social structure. To make this possible, it was sufficient that only a minority of the population married, because every marriage was the basis of a household with a great many unmarried members: children, brothers, sisters, uncles, aunts, manservants, maidservants, journeymen, apprentices. In the modern age of organizations everyone must be a person if he is to occupy his position in the social structure. For this he needs a place where he is acknowledged as a person and can live as a person. That place is the modern family. But the composition of the family — the ideal type consisting only of parents and growing children — means that the adult needs a family of his own. It was therefore wholly consistent that the great upheaval in the nineteenth century should bring with it the basic claim by every adult to the right to marry. Today more than ninety percent of all adults over thirty-five are married, widowed, or divorced. But when this legitimate universal demand for a place where one is accepted as a person and not subjected to demands for achievement is not met, there is a yawning gap. As celibacy in our time is uncommon, it is a different matter and at the same time more burdensome than in the era of the stratified society; then it was the fate of many people, perhaps the majority, and was accepted as a matter of course. This gap can and must be closed in some way or other for the persons concerned; and there are ways in which it can be done, especially through friendship, another personal relationship that was discovered and consciously transfigured at the same time — and not coincidentally — as was the love match. Often, too, it may be possible for the unmarried person to associate with another family; but any such association requires an understanding on both sides and continual watchfulness and detachment, in view of the ease with which personal family life can be disturbed, and any relationship that does not rest either on marriage or on kinship has an unstable basis.

We must still devote some attention here to a role of special importance played by the family in modern society. The family is the place par excellence where those "conserving powers" referred to by Hans Freyer are cultivated and passed on. The upbringing that takes place in the family mediates more effectively than other institutions all that still remains to us of chivalry, the old rural ethos, integrity, the patrician style of wealthy old families, and things of that kind. It is a precious heritage, and it is no longer being renewed, because the old institutions that created and disseminated it have passed away; but it still helps to support and stabilize our open and vulnerable world. Its influence remains, too, in public life, in business, and in government; but now it hardly reaches the rising generations except through the hidden channels of family upbringing, through the personal action of parents in their teaching and example. Thus the family stands in the midst of the world of organizations, a stranger and yet of the same kin, different in kind but in its own special way profoundly essential to the survival and stability of the whole.

When the old household dissolved, with the members of the family going their different ways and the old authoritarian pattern inevitably coming to an end, there were loud cries of warning: "The family is disappearing. Save the family!" And the Soviet system really believed, in its early period, that the family was a relic of a bygone time, and that it had to be dissolved and eliminated; it tried to create an all-embracing organization in the form of the machinery of the state, and to draw the upbringing of children wholly into its orbit. The attempt failed, and the cries of warning proved to have been precipitate and to have misinterpreted the historical development. Today the Soviet Union has actually turned its attention to protecting the family. The experience of Germans after the collapse in 1945 demonstrated that if all organizations, including the state, break down, then the family, including the wider circle of relatives, is still there ready to help.

It requires little imagination to see how things are going to proceed in China. In that country, too, an attempt has been made to replace domestic life by an organization known as the "people's commune." Sooner or later this futile attempt will also have to be abandoned. Of course, we must remember that after its own unsuccessful effort the Soviet Union did not simply revert to the old kind of family. That had been a particular kind of "household," namely, an extended family, which was inadequate to the demands of modern industrial society. What exists there today is the modern small family. In the same way, the Chinese large family of the old style was not flexible, mobile, and personal, but rigidly static and institutional. Today the Chinese are developing the modern industrial society as fast as they can, and wherever it has made progress in China, it has already produced the small family of the modern type.

12

Faith and Church in

the Modern World

In a single book, especially in a book of such limited scope as the present one, it is impossible to deal, step by step, with the whole area of the subject under discussion. Modern society is an immense and extremely diverse structure, and at best we can only point out salient features, lines of connection, and structural patterns. Our presentation of the subject has been limited to a sketch of one central question: the basic institutional relationships of our time. From this central point the lines radiate out into all the spheres of our economic and social life, including — to mention only a few — questions of education, the use of leisure, and consumers' interests.

In this last chapter we want to sum up the matter, not by writing a formal summary of our conclusions, but by looking at the question of the church in modern society. For it is on that question that those lines just mentioned converge. Our reflections on the church come at the end of the book, because our whole discussion thus far points in this direction. We conclude our discussion, then, by considering two concepts: the concept of history, specifically, the Christian view of history; and the concept of the church,[1] specifically, the shape that the church

[1] [The author treats *Kirche* and *Gemeinde* as equivalent concepts (see p. 194 below); accordingly, we render both words as "church," or, sometimes, as "the (Christian) community." — TRANS.]

assumes and the way it regards itself in an environment consisting of organizations and small families.

History and the Person

Our discussion set in at the point of the downgrading of the sacrosanct order of things which up until that time had encompassed and guided man's life. Through a unique and unprecedented call "from beyond," man saw himself translated into a new status, a threefold dialectical relationship — to God, to the other person, and to himself. To designate this status, we have here been using a nonbiblical word: person. As the gospel soberly predicted, it was a more-than-ordinary demand. The comprehensive claim, "You, therefore, must be perfect, as your heavenly Father is perfect" (Matt. 5:48), was bound to extend beyond those to whom it was first addressed. They remained harnessed, as it were, to two facts: they continued to belong to historical institutions, and they could not, in their own strength, fulfil their role as persons. That fulfillment they awaited in a new aeon that lay beyond history but had already dawned; as Christians they were citizens of their existing households and states, and yet they stood apart from them in a different existence and a different relation to time.

A thousand years were to pass before a new social pattern commensurate with this twofold existence began to emerge from it; it was a social pattern which referred those who stood within it to a personal existence beyond its boundaries and which even found that personal existence necessary to its own existence. We have followed ordinary usage in speaking of this new social structure as "organization." It was almost another thousand years before the new structure had fully developed and established itself in the Christian nations generally. Today all public life in the old industrial countries is based on this principle, and family life has been shaped accordingly. Security of existence depends almost entirely on the efficient functioning of the new structure. The other peoples of the world are at various stages along the path to entrusting their fate to the same structure.

What we have seen of the fully developed organization has shown that the main responsibility for its continued virile existence already rests on man's existence as a person, and that everything points to his having to bear this load increasingly in the future. According to the structural realities, this responsibility laid on the person is characterized by a threefold dialectical relationship that refers to its point of origin. First it is rooted in and related to the "situation," which represents the whole network of world affairs as these bear on a particular person at a given moment. Secondly, it is related to the other person as partner. And thirdly, it stands in relation to oneself. What is very disturbing, however, is that we can again see here the immensity of the demand, and that the structure itself has laid on man insistent claims to which, with his known strength, he does not feel equal. At the same time, the security of existence itself is coming to depend increasingly on whether these claims are met.

Thus the present personal claim refers back to its point of origin, and so, in fact, to the forces there which are suprahistorical yet have entered into history. They were concentrated, and remain so for all time, in the figure of him who not only taught personal existence but lived it and, according to his words, will always do so. It was he who put the threefold personal existence into a terse formula and described it as "the great and first commandment" on which, together with the "second . . . like it," "depend all the law and the prophets" (Matt. 22:38–40), that is, the whole basic structure of existence, which he had come in order to "fulfil": "You shall love the Lord your *God* with all your heart, and with all your soul, and with all your mind, and your *neighbor* as *yourself*" (Matt. 22:34–40; Mark 12:28–31; Luke 10:25–27). That is the threefold relationship, life in all its breadth, which a man can meet only with his whole being; and that is love, the inexpressible force that alone "fulfils" every given relationship.

The church later accepted dialectical personal existence as the basis of faith as a whole, inasmuch as it divided the confession of faith into three articles, one for each of the three "persons" of the triune God.

In the person of Christ man appeared as a "person" in purity, and it is in and through him that God has called all men to live as persons. This means that there irrupted into the world a transforming event, the historical results of which must be evident even to the nonbeliever. The historical results, however, have been that the world has assumed a pattern that points insistently to this pure person, not merely as someone who made an impact long ago, but as someone who is awaited at this present time. Thus our attention is again directed to the Living One who said, "I am with you always, to the close of the age" (Matt. 28:20), and who predicted, "Apart from me you can do nothing" (John 15:5). And the fact that the demand for pure personal existence is not only urgent, but becoming ever more urgent, points to the same figure for the third time, to the figure of the Coming One, "who is and who was and who is to come" (Rev. 1:4, etc.).

Today there are two serious hindrances to allowing ourselves to proceed from a given set of empirically demonstrable findings to affirmations made by Christian faith. Both are quite legitimate and must not be ignored or dismissed. One is the distrust of a "natural theology" that would explain the appearance of Christ on the basis of man's inexorable development to a constantly higher pattern of life. This concern is justified, for it represents an attempt to adapt the Christian confession of faith to a way of thinking which is scientific or scientifically determined, a way of thinking that is already discredited in science itself. The Christian confession of faith is here objectivized, and therefore vitiated from the outset.

The second hindrance is a satiation with historical theories which seek to locate the Christian consummation of history within the course of history and which see the world as progressing upward by stages toward a radiant end. The conceptions of history in German idealism, or the socialist utopias, or the very banal ideas of progress current in the nineteenth and early twentieth centuries, or the ideology of the Third Reich, or the Russian messianic consciousness, of which Bolshevism was simply the latest expression — these things represented, and still represent, such views of history. Earlier examples are to be found within the church itself, particularly in the speculative expectations and historical systematizing of Abbot Joachim of Fiore (or Flora) in the twelfth century. Today we find such theorizing about the course of world history intolerable; disastrous blows have brought us down to earth from our optimism about progress, and messianic ideologies have brought us great suffering.

The rejection of both of these approaches to history is fully justified, for in neither case have they helped us to understand world history or contributed anything of value to our approach to the Christian faith. Therefore, any rigorous critique that sharpens our intellectual awareness in this respect can only be welcomed.

Today, however, we are threatened by new dangers from other directions. In trying to avoid these two false paths, people are, on the one hand, blind to obvious and irreversible currents of world history, and belittle them; on the other hand, the realm of faith is completely detached from actual happenings and ends up in sterile isolation.

There is no doubt that world history is moving in certain directions, some of which have been discussed in this book: the dismantling of sacrosanct traditional orders and institutions, and their disenchantment and secularization; the transition to a general flexibility of men, things, patterns of life, and modes of conduct; in harmony with all this, the structuring of life along organizational lines; and finally the realization of the importance of the person, even though at first this may often be masked and only indirectly attested by conscious and brutal repression of the person, for existence as a person can be purposefully attacked only where the conception of personal existence is already there in principle, even as the same presupposition is needed for the attack to be experienced as painful. All of these currents are irreversible, and one cannot in the long run get back behind them. What is happening is something irrevocable, and it is happening today in and to all the nations of the earth; that is, it is truly and conclusively "world" history.

These are great, sweeping currents of world history. They

too, however, are the result of that transforming irruption into history two thousand years ago, which occurred, not at any chance time or place, but "when the time was fulfilled" (Mark 1:15), when much had already preceded to prepare and show the way. And the person who was the chosen instrument of that irruption has promised to return at the end of history. So when an historical theory that takes account only of the course of our world's affairs comes to grief, the place from which we can and must look at history in its entirety is here: in Christ's coming, in what he accomplished, and in the expectation of his return. Unless we look to him, we cannot see history in its true light and we belie our own reckoning of time, in which every date, whether in history or at the head of any business letter, refers to the birth of Christ as the pivotal point of world history.

On the other hand, if we claim to live a life of Christian faith without regard or reference to world history, it means that we do not believe the words of the gospel itself. The references to the "fulfilled" time (Mark 1:15; Gal. 4:4), and to a future filled with political, economic, and natural catastrophes, are explicit enough; and it is all related to the coming and the return of the "Son of man," and to the preaching of the "gospel of the kingdom . . . throughout the whole world, as a testimony to all nations" (Matt. 24:14).

Thus, if we rightly reject historical systems that take account solely of this world, we must nonetheless — if we relate world history to the person of Christ — come back to the gospel itself and to the authentic idea of history directed toward a goal. For "a Christian interpretation of history is fixed on the future as the temporal horizon of a definite purpose and goal; and all modern attempts to delineate history as a meaningful, though indefinite, progress toward fulfillment depend on this theological thought."[2] In ancient times there was the "classical notion of time as an eternal cycle."[3] Time was then generally reckoned from some exceptionally important political event, such as the

---

[2] Karl Löwith, *Meaning in History: The Theological Implications of the Philosophy of History* (Chicago: University of Chicago Press, 1949), p. 160.
[3] *Ibid.*

founding of Rome, or the first Olympic Games as an event that concerned the whole of Greece. Later the Jewish-Christian world introduced a time scheme of an entirely new kind which covered the whole of time and the whole world. "For the Christian the dividing line in the history of salvation is no longer a mere *futurum,* but a *perfectum praesens,* the accomplished advent of Jesus Christ. With regard to this central event the time is reckoned *forward as well as backward* . . . . In this linear, but centered, movement a progressive condensation and reduction takes place, culminating in the single representative figure of Christ, to be followed by a progressive expansion of the central event into a world-wide community of believers, who live in and through Christ . . . ."[4]

On one important point, however, we must take definite exception to the book from which we have just quoted, although at just this point it expresses a generally held conviction: "As a history of the world, the empirical history after Christ is qualitatively not different from the history before Christ if judged from either a strictly empirical or a strictly Christian viewpoint . . . . In its profane appearance it [history] is a continuous repetition of painful miscarriages and costly achievements which end in ordinary failures . . . ."[5] Of course, history after Christ too is a constant repetition of efforts and failures, but even empirically it is more than that. The onesided emphasis on meaningless repetition is an expression of disappointment with all theories of progress, whether sublime or banal, but it is an emphasis that is still in thrall to such theories. For in this respect those who believe in progress are like those who deny that the world has been changed by Christianity — they all think that if the world is to be permanently changed, it must be through improvement, through "successes," and through a gradual approach to the goal. But this tacit assumption is nowhere substantiated, least of all in the words of the gospel itself, which expressly warns us of the consequences that were bound to follow upon the proclamation

[4] *Ibid.,* p. 182.
[5] *Ibid.,* p. 190.

of the gospel: "Do not give dogs what is holy; and do not throw your pearls before swine, lest they trample them under foot and turn to attack you" (Matt. 7:6). To whatever peoples the gospel came, it broke up their long-established sacrosanct orders and institutions; and this happened repeatedly even where these had been set up under Christian auspices. That has resulted in increasing unrest and outward insecurity in the world. A Christianity that thought in terms of established orders overlooked the fact that alongside the gospel's claim to be solid rock for the foundation of a house stood its claim to possess explosive power: "Do you think that I have come to give peace on earth? No, I tell you, but rather division; for henceforth in one house there will be five divided, three against two and two against three" (Luke 12:51–52).

The fact that the gospel has loosed human existence from the institutional principle and entrusted it to that of personal responsibility has meant a growing insecurity and a loss of stability. Ultimately it has meant the emergence of an entirely new structural principle — the organization — which is adapted to personal responsibility and which consciously or unconsciously wants, demands, and presupposes such responsibility. The "organization" has not yet succeeded in making the world peaceful and secure again, and it may be doubted whether it will ever be able to do so.

In view of these facts, one can no longer say that "history after Christ is qualitatively not different from the history before Christ." It is true that the qualitative difference has not meant that the world has been christianized in the sense of being improved and made pacific. It has brought the perplexity, the lack of peace, the disorder that Christ himself said he would bring — indeed, would have to bring — for the sake of the ultimate end. Many of his sayings and parables are meant to prepare people for that.

Moreover, there is a qualitative difference in the manner and the causes of the disorder. It is true that many things remain the same as before; they existed in ancient times and will always exist: love of power, vanity, cruelty, envy, hatred.

191

But today they are mingled with motives and aims of a quite specific kind, and they employ new methods which involve more than a mere quantitative increase of effectiveness. The specifically new element is the attack on the person. That is what we feel to be the really agonizing and satanic thing, the perverse and deadly element. What perplexes us today is not the mere fact of murder, however horrible it is, nor even the mere fact of mass murder, however ghastly it is. It is the fact that in murder, in mass murder by sophisticated apparatuses — gas chambers, saturation bombing, or intercontinental missiles — the demonic itself is at work. The crux of the matter here is not that man kills man, as Cain killed Abel, but that man is denied recognition as a person and is snuffed out like a vermin. And this kind of annihilation is simply the final stage in the disintegration of the person, when in a pluralistic and diversified world based on organizations and on persons as persons, wholesale judgments are pronounced that deal in black-and-white categories: "the" Soviets, "the" Jews, "the" Germans, "the" West, "the" free world. The disintegration then proceeds to forcible conformity, accusations of collective guilt, truth serums, brainwashing, and so on. What we regard with horror in such things is the threat to, or the elimination of, the person, since the machinery, the "secondary system," is in fact functioning automatically, reducing man to a function, or, if that fails, eliminating him. We shudder to think that the personal existence with which man has been endowed during two thousand years of Christian history has become so vulnerable in the last few decades that it can be seized and destroyed.

This is the same personal existence which is demanded of us in the small as well as in the great situations of our lives and which in our constitutional rights is regarded as a precious possession, but which we nevertheless feel to be so heavy and burdensome that we repeatedly take refuge from it in excuses and collective expedients. Thus it is that we say that in the background of all historical epochs there stands — waiting, working, and weighing, and always visible to one who has eyes to see — the figure of him who was wholly and completely a person, praying to God, at one with his neighbor, and yet the "wholly other" before him, exercising self-control. He is equal to every situation, for in him "are hid all the treasures of wisdom and knowledge" (Col. 2:3) and to him is given "all authority in heaven and on earth" (Matt. 28:18). But the way his knowledge and authority triumphed was through death, death in the name of and at the hands of the institution, which regarded itself as sacrosanct. He is still dying that death today.

The humanitarian protest against our present-day "inhumanity" and its instruments is good and right and necessary, but as long as it remains nothing more than disillusioned faith in progress it does not go to the root of what is happening here. The expression "relapse into barbarism" visualizes world history in terms of the "march of civilization," and by so doing remains superficial. That is the reason, too, why the humanitarian protest is so illuminating and yet so ineffective. Of course we must try by every feasible means to improve our civilization, but unless our gaze and our understanding penetrate more deeply than this, we are bound to be faced with one disappointment after another. For the "barbarism" of our own days is something quite different from the condition of primitive peoples before the dawn of civilization. Today's barbarism is human guilt itself, erupting and overpowering men; it is the person, emancipated and grown to maturity and responsibility, now choosing to ignore both the call that brought him into the world and the goal that was set before him: personal responsibility to God and to his neighbor. No such tests were imposed on man by the world of orders and institutions, for then the institutions assumed the responsibility in his stead. Today, in a world based on organizations, man bears the responsibility himself, as a person, in the way initiated by the gospel. And as the gospel plainly foresaw, personal responsibility is too heavy to be borne by man in history, and the road takes him through crises that become increasingly severe. But the same gospel tells us that this road is, in the end, the way to fulfillment. That is known only to faith, but it is from faith that personal existence comes, and it is to faith that it must turn.

The Church as "Organization"

In the painful and strenuous efforts by the church and by Christian congregations to understand and reshape themselves in the modern world, we can see today all the anxieties and labors that exist in the church — all the doubts and questions, the uncertainties and experiments, the loyalty to tradition and the fresh starts. No question in the church is unrelated to these efforts, and everything that we shall consider here has deep roots in the past. The whole of our foregoing discussion would trail off into oblivion if it did not lead up to this question. In the present context it will suffice to regard church and congregation as equivalent concepts, and to ignore their differences and demarcations. Moreover, this many-faceted and involved complex of questions can be treated here only from one angle. It is impossible even to touch on the new issues that have arisen in connection with them. We can only pick up from our previous discussion a few of the threads that lead in this direction and here converge in new conclusions.

We first have to recognize that the church, following in the wake of the general transition from the principle of "order" or "institution" to that of "organization," has itself taken on features of an organization. As a social entity it has been compelled to adapt itself to the world of organizations.

In the traditional world of the Middle Ages, in spite of the kaleidoscopic variety of social structures, there was no "pluralism." All the individual entities fitted — at any rate in theory — into a great comprehensive *ordo,* in which the church occupied an important focal position, intimately intermeshed with every facet of the social realm. In the course of the dissolution of that world, the church's ties with the social fabric were severed one by one, and it came to stand, more and more, by itself. In the nineteenth century the old system of feudal institutions and brotherhoods disappeared, and the organizations that emerged in their place were as a matter of course "secular" and alien to the church. The entity with which the church remained linked the longest was the one that ended up as the only one claiming to be an "order": the state. But even the alliance of church and state was finally dissolved, even in most European countries, and with that the church was finally thrown back on itself; it became one social entity among many others, a constituent part of the universal pluralism.

In this situation, connected in a variety of ways with other organizations and supported by people whose outlook was shaped by the organization, the church itself has assumed, in its outward image, the characteristics of an organization.[6] The Protestant churches have become organizations insofar as their forms and structures have become more flexible. Forms of thought, of proclamation, of worship, of congregational structure, of church government, having lost the once undisputed sanction of tradition, have been refashioned, or have completely disappeared, or have changed their significance. Entirely new structures have been devised and developed, such as the church auxiliaries, social work, and so on. There is no need to go into details. Having developed this flexibility of new and creative approaches, ecclesiastical forms shook off a sacrosanct rigidity that had already appeared in Protestantism in spite of its doctrines and the influence of the Reformation. The forms were stripped of their sanctity and secularized, in line with the gospel and the Reformation.

The flexibility of forms, however, brings up the question of aims. An organization's outward form is, or ought to be, determined by its aims. The form is changed if new circumstances arise which make it necessary to pursue the aims in a new way; and the same holds good for the church, insofar as it has become an organization. The church has, in fact, changed its forms and structures and is still doing so continually, since the

---

[6] We are referring here to the Protestant churches. In Roman Catholicism, which even today retains much more of the claim to be an "order," but which at the same time takes account of modern conditions, things are different in many respects.

circumstances in which it pursues its aims have indeed become quite different, and will in all probability go on changing. The world is on the move, and so the church is too, insofar as it is an historical phenomenon. For the purpose of the church is to be in the world and carry out the commission entrusted to it by Jesus Christ: "Go therefore and make disciples of all nations, baptizing them in the name of the Father and of the Son and of the Holy Spirit, teaching them to observe all that I have commanded you" (Matt. 28:19–20).

Regarding the new circumstances in which the old command is to be carried out, we would point, by way of illustration, to three very significant facts. First, the church can no longer be constituted so as to embrace and determine the whole of life, as it used to. To that extent, too, the church has become an organization. Even in early modern times the fact that a member of a congregation was barred from the altar meant that he was ostracized by other citizens. Church discipline was exercised in the context of the surveillance that governed one's whole existence in one's station in life and in one's neighborhood; the public denunciation of wrongdoing from the pulpit was a means of discipline that was generally employed, accepted on principle, and effective. But in our world of organizations, which has had to develop a carefully sealed-off "private life" and can no longer recognize any right of public interference in personal questions, the presuppositions for the old kind of "church discipline" do not exist. Any attempt to reintroduce them would only cause annoyance and alienate people from the church. The church, like all organizations, has been given well-defined limits with respect to the extent to which it may include people within its sphere. Thus the church, too, is included in the universal pluralism of the social spheres which, while they compete with each other for influence on people, always have to respect each person's responsibility for himself. Tutelage is no longer tolerated anywhere.

Secondly — and this is implicit in what has just been said — the church has not kept pace with developments emanating from its own message. Within the church there is a widespread conviction, held to be almost self-evident, that most people in the Christian nations have more or less relinquished their connection with the church, and that the church's efforts must therefore be directed toward winning them back. It is very important that the church today realize that this conviction does not correspond to reality, for we have here the reason why so many painstaking efforts produce such small results. The theory of "apostasy" regards the present time as "unchristian," ignoring its Christian origin and its hidden core of Christianity. But if we recognize the validity of our discussion, we can see that it is not that the modern world has fallen away from the church, but that the church has not sufficiently pursued the ramifications of its own message. The world is not commissioned to follow after the church; on the contrary, the church is commissioned to follow after the world, and on a path that it has itself prepared. If the "world's" structures — desacralized, pluralistic, adapted to the organization and to personal responsibility — have grown from a Christian root, the church must be all the more ready to show the same characteristics in its own structures and to foster mature, personal responsibility. The more this is the case, the better will be the conditions for handing on its "teaching" to the modern world — that is, for fulfilling its purpose as an organization.

Thirdly, entirely new circumstances have arisen that affect the church's mission to non-Christian peoples. In fact, this may well constitute the most provocative question the Christian church faces today. For if within the Christian nations developments emanating from the gospel have outpaced developments in the church itself, how much more is that the case among the non-Christian, predominantly dark-skinned peoples of the earth. Today they too are caught up in the process of industrialization and modernization on a grand scale. They are all being brought under the influence of the organizational pattern. In all of them, ancient traditions are disintegrating, and on all sides patterns of life are being desacralized and laid open to the grip of objectivity. That often takes place, as in China, through ruthless collectivist procedures that show no respect for personality. And yet these very procedures that so mercilessly annihilate the person betray at the same time an awareness of the person. Europeans ought to know, with their fund of experience, that such happenings are an indication of the shape of the future. For the organization needs the person and presupposes his existence. That is in the nature of the case. In the early period of the organization in the West, only one individual or a few in the leadership were "persons." But those in the leadership have never been able anywhere, in the long run, to monopolize the privilege of existence as a person and the making of decisions based on the facts at hand. The pressure of the facts compels the extension of that privilege, the more complex and mobile the world of organizations becomes in a technological age. That is already becoming evident in the Soviet Union, which has taken the logical step, namely, increased decentralization.

The provocative question that now arises is this: How is the need of the non-Christian peoples for personal existence to be met? The gospel and a long churchly tradition have given to the Christian nations certain categories which are helpful to them in implementing the implications of the Christian faith. Most of us, when we see the need for personal existence and find people clamoring for acceptance as persons, know the meaning and dynamics of personal responsibility in terms of its very wellspring. We have even preserved among us an ancient Christian "legacy" (in Hans Freyer's sense) which the demands of the new situation can summon and stir. But what about the non-Christian peoples? What are they to do about their need for personal existence? It is here that collectivist ideologies come up against their own limitations. What resources are the industrialized peoples of Asia and Africa to draw upon? What conceptual forms will they employ in meeting a need imposed on them too by the sheer pressure of the facts, the need for personal existence which was pioneered for them too by the Christian faith?

This is the question. And it would be wishful thinking at this point to suggest what the answer will be. We can predict nothing. The most we can do is to wait and see what develops. All the same, the question is of the utmost importance for the Christian church today, if it is to "go . . . and make disciples of all nations," for the nations are all at one stage or another of the process of industrialization. We have here two entities forced into mutual relationship: on the one hand, the nations that are being increasingly pushed by the industrializing and organizing process into that personal existence which is of Christian origin, and, on the other hand, the church, which is to go to these, as to all nations, and impart that personal existence. That has been its commission from the very beginning, and if it fails in this, it is not living up to its own nature. The course of history suggests that a bridge may here be built, indeed that its piers have already been laid.

Personal Life — Fashioned in the Church

Now that we have made it sufficiently clear that the church itself, being in an organizational world, has features of an organization determined by its purposes, we must be equally careful to emphasize that the church is not an organization in the proper sense of the term. As so often happens in the modern world, we again have to keep two contradictory facts in mind at the same time.

An organization is a social structure that takes for granted and uses, for its own maintenance, personal resources that are outside it and essentially different from it. That is the characteristic on which we have based our account of the organization. But that particular characteristic does not hold good in the case of the church. The forces that sustain the church are not contributed from outside but live within the church itself. That is shown by the fact that the church's commission, its "purpose" as an organization (as was noted earlier), is followed by the promise: "And lo, I am with you always, to the close of the age." These words are spoken, not by just anyone, but by the Son of man, who lived in purity the life of personal existence that he had brought into the world and who will live it "to the close of the age." He is the ever-present force at work in the believing community, "For where two or three are gathered in my name, there am I in the midst of them" (Matt. 18:20). No organization has such a lasting foundation; and a structure that has such a force inherent in it is not merely an organization, but something more and different. In this difference resides the church's unique nature, which in the modern world, as indeed in all ages, gives it its special position and special task.

The essence of this distinctive characteristic is that in the church personal existence lives and works, that is, a structure is erected and a relationship to reality is established and lived that cannot be erected, established, or lived anywhere else.

We can best make this clear by going back for a moment to Christian beginnings. In the historical sphere, the uniqueness of the Christian community lay in its startling abolition of life's hitherto-accepted foundations. All sanctity that derived from hearth and home, from family and ancestry, from race, city, kingdom and empire, was broken down, and man was confronted with the eternal creator, God, who alone was holy. The world's orders and institutions were relativized; they lost their unconditionally binding character. Further, the accepted relationship to the other man was disrupted in two ways. First, the individual was loosed from his unconditional, existential ties with his relatives, clansmen, and fellow citizens, and was placed ultimately, as an individual on his own account, before God — everyone in the same way, whether master or slave, Greek or Jew, man or woman. Secondly, the individual was taken out of his unconditional, existential separation from his "enemy," from the stranger, from the barbarian, and this other person was entrusted to him existentially as one who could always be his neighbor. Here man was at last placed under a self-surveillance governed by standards which were diametrically opposed to the hitherto-accepted standards of institutional surveillance by one's kin, tribe, city, or state, and which therefore thwarted and relativized those traditional standards.

Thus the founding of the Christian community meant that a

completely new mode of life in the world was established; in that community this mode of life was handed on and continually renewed. This mode of life is the personal existence of which we have been speaking. It is an existence that cannot be supported and lived by the isolated individual, for "the person" is more than the individual. By virtue of his nature, he is related to his origin in the gospel and to the goal at the end of history; thus he stands in the context of a tradition and a future expectation. So the personal mode of life in the world is fashioned and lived in the Christian community.

For two thousand years the Christian community has worked as leaven in the world. During that time it has changed the world qualitatively to a very high degree. If in its beginnings it appeared as something new and disturbing, a force that broke up and wrecked the existing foundations, it has since produced in and from itself a world which is left with no other foundations and which is always sent back to it as the only foundation there is.

Our world of today is so constructed that all objects and all relationships can and must be dealt with objectively. There is no retreat from this; but now it is vital that this "objectivity" keep, or acquire, that open and all-embracing character that is proper to it. Any absolutizing of strictly immanent values leads to pernicious distortions and short-circuits, whether those values represent state or nation, socialism or capitalism, tradition or progress, earnings or security, democracy or bolshevism. It was belief in an eternal God that first freed the world from all absolutisms. Today the world cannot endure unless it remains free from them, or, rather, unless it is continually being freed from them. The church's vision and life are inseparably linked with that origin and that foundation.

Moreover, our world of today is so constructed that, although each of us stands alone in his own particular situation, at the same time we live in an "unusual intensity of interdependence" at every turn, and equality of rights has become in law and practice an unconditional prerequisite for the proper functioning of our organizations. Again the Christian faith, which has opened the way for this detachment, has also shown us the bridge across to the stranger, the alien, and even to the enemy, and has carried into the world the revolutionary idea of the equality of all as "equality before God." Here, too, the Christian community's vision and life — a "life in Christ" — are inseparably linked with the origin and foundation of that changed world.

Then, too, the world is so constructed that, while institutional surveillance and self-surveillance exist side by side, each with its own standards, we are moving increasingly in the direction of the latter. It was the gospel that first brought to man as a possibility this detached and surveillant attitude toward himself, in all its depth and rigor, and at the same time provided the new standards that were needed. Again, there is no turning back from this, but everything depends on whether this self-surveillance is exercised rightly and effectively. Again it is the church that keeps alive our knowledge of the permanent source and the valid standards.

Thus the Christian community, with what it is and stands for, is not on the periphery of modern society, but at its very center. It has no islands to defend and save; its own being is the foundation for the material of which and on which the modern world is being built.

That certainly means that, as far as its own shape is concerned, the Christian community can no longer be thought of, or built up, along the lines of a "church order" that keeps people in its tutelage; rather, it must be directed toward mature men of personal responsibility. In the church the efforts to press forward in this direction are increasing, and they are increasingly vocal. It is significant that Dietrich Bonhoeffer's call for a "religionless Christianity" and for openness toward "a world come of age" has evoked so great a response.

However, all this does not alter the fact that the Christian community, even if it finds the shape appropriate for the modern world, is always something "wholly other," even more so than when it appeared in the Jewish-Hellenistic-Roman world and later spread among the Germanic, Celtic, Slavic, and nonwhite peoples. Seen historically, its views and standards are utopian. Its faith for the future envisages the end of history, not some coming historical epoch. Because it knows this, historical catastrophes mean for it not a disappointed faith in human progress, but a confirmation of its knowledge of guilt and the cross. Here again, it roots its outlook and its life in a deeper reality.

When "sovereigns" were still the only ones who made the decisions on matters affecting the people, the world recoiled from its oppressive discovery that political (that is, objective, organizational) action was inevitably tainted with guilt. Machiavelli was the first to recognize and express this clearly; and all responsible statesmen after him have come to realize, either cynically or with an uneasy conscience, that there is no escape from guilt in dealing with the sovereign affairs of state. The old message of the gospel, repeated by Luther in deep dismay, was experienced here first of all by a small stratum of responsible people. Whoever experienced it in faith knew that political rule "by God's grace" was no empty slogan.

Today it is not only state sovereignty and responsibility for political action that have been transferred to the great mass of the population; we have also all become involved in decision-making based on the facts at hand, without the benefit of any unconditionally valid tradition. The heavy burden of inescapable guilt has thus been transferred from the shoulders of kings to our own shoulders.

People are not yet generally aware of this, however, and on all sides there are well-intended efforts to achieve a this-worldly perfectionism, in politics, economics, education, and so on. Where the inescapability of guilt is recognized and experienced, however, there are three possible courses open. First, one may bow to the inevitable with a cynicism that allows nothing to stand in the way of violent action; the recent past, as well as the present, provides us with plenty of examples. Secondly, "conserving powers" from past times, also lacking in depth of insight, may ward off the worst of the evils; but that is uncertain ground, and it becomes less and less certain with every decade that takes us further from the orders and institutions of the past. Thirdly, the inescapability of guilt may be experienced within the Christian community. Here is to be found the forgiveness of guilt, the only living force which can again and again break the deadly chain of guilt, reprisal, and counterreprisal, even within history. Today the world is everywhere caught in the grip of such a chain, and there are no organizational means in sight that by themselves can really break it. With God's forgiveness and men's forgiveness towards one another, however, there takes place in the Christian community an event of the greatest personal importance, an event which, despite all deadly chains, can always enable us to make a fresh start.

Index

Index

INDEX

God, x, xi, 186, 187, 200, 201, 204
  grace of, 203
  personal, 12, 14, 19
Goethe, *Die natürliche Tochter,* 163
Gospel, the Christian, 7, 25, 27, 38,
  47, 54, 62, 185, 190, 191, 193,
  195, 202, 203
Gospels, the, x, 18
Greeks, 26
Greek thought, 148
Gregory VII, 48–50
Grönbeck, Wilhelm, 30, 58
Group ties, 90–91
Guilds, 85–86, 90, 116
Guilt, 193, 203–204

"Hawthorne experiment," 108
Hegel, 59
  Philosophy of Right, 129–131, 136
Heraclitus, 28
Herberg, Will, x
History, 2–3
  Christian, 192
  goal of, 20, 24
  law of, 167
  and person, 185–193
  social, 28
  views of
    biblical, 3, 187–188
    Christian, 189, 193
    world, 188–190
Hohenzollerns, 56
Household, 66–68, 87, 90, 97, 99,
  101, 138, 173–175, 176, 181

Idealism, 147
Ideas, 87–88
Ideologies, 87–89, 188
Impersonality, vii
Individual, the, viii, 13, 127, 140–
  141, 146; *see also* Person; Man
  and association, 83–84
  and God, 14–15, 19, 28
  Greek view of, 49
  and institution, 32, 58, 86
  liberation of, 25–27, 53, 59
  and organization; *see* Organiza-
    tion, and person

Individualism, 27, 88
Individualization, 107, 144, 146
Individualizing process, 74
Industrial concern, 98
Industrialization, 2–3, 61, 65, 199
Industrial Revolution, 6, 61
Industrial society, 61, 98, 111, 183
Institution
  and association, 82–83
  dismantling of, 55–60, 74
  and freedom, 49
  inviolable (sacrosanct), ix–x, 12,
    121
  and Jewish law, 8–12
  legal basis of, 58–59
  and organization, 145–146
  and person (individual), 18–23,
    30–39, 66, 86–87, 126, 148–
    149, 176; *see also* Individual,
    and institution
  and social life, 130
Interests, 133–136
Italy, 51

Jerusalem, 15, 16
Jesus; *see* Christ, Jesus
Joachim, Abbot of Fiore, 188
Job(s); *see* Work
Judaism, 13
Judgment, x, 16

Kern, Fritz, 31
Killing, 9, 15, 192
Kingdom of God, 14, 21, 24
Kolb, William, x

Labor unions, 92
Landmarks of Tomorrow; see
  Drucker, Peter
Law (Jewish), 8–13, 18–19, 30, 32
Law(s), 34, 49, 58, 121
  equality under, 100
  rule of, 120
Lebensraum, 76, 78–80, 81
Lenski, Gerhard, x
Libertarianism, 133–141
Life
  bipolar structure of, 28